THE BEGINNER'S GUIDE TO ALCHEMY

Practical Lessons and Exercises
to Enhance Your Life

THE BEGINNER'S GUIDE TO
ALCHEMY

SARAH DURN

ROCKRIDGE
PRESS

For general information on our other products and services or to obtain technical support, please contact our Customer Care Department within the United States at (866) 744-2665, or outside the United States at (510) 253-0500.

Rockridge Press publishes its books in a variety of electronic and print formats. Some content that appears in print may not be available in electronic books, and vice versa.

TRADEMARKS: Rockridge Press and the Rockridge Press logo are trademarks or registered trademarks of Callisto Media Inc. and/or its affiliates, in the United States and other countries, and may not be used without written permission. All other trademarks are the property of their respective owners. Rockridge Press is not associated with any product or vendor mentioned in this book.

Interior and Cover Designer: Jay Dea
Art Producer: Samantha Ulban
Editor: Jesse Aylen
Production Editor: Jenna Dutton

Shutterstock/Morphart Creation, p.5; iStock/ilbusca, p.7; Shutterstock/Kristina Vor, p.11; Shutterstock/Natata, p.28, 104; ART Collection/Alamy, p.33; Topham Partners LLP/Alamy, p.34, 72, 79; The History Collection/Alamy, p.36; The Reading Room/Alamy, top left p.37; FALKENSTEINFOTO/Alamy, bottom right p.37; Historic Images/Alamy, p.46; The Picture Art Collection/Alamy, p.49; Classic Collection/Alamy, p.54; Art Collection 2/Alamy, p.62; Welcome Collection, p.92; Shutterstock/Naci Yavuz, p.94; Art Heritage/Alamy, p.98; Shuterstock/Artur Balytski, p.106, Creative Market/Pixejoo, cover and all other art. Author photo courtesy of © Evlin Lake.

ISBN: Print 978-1-64611-747-5
       eBook 978-1-64611-748-2
R0

To my mother, who always
knew I'd accomplish the Great
Work that is one's first book, and
to my dad, for always telling
me how proud he is of me.

CONTENTS

INTRODUCTION

WELCOME TO THE WONDROUS WORLD OF ALCHEMY! I couldn't be more pleased to share with you this strange pocket of knowledge I've accumulated through the years. It's a pocket of insight and wonder that has transformed how I see the world.

My fascination with alchemy began with a long drive from Ohio to Maine and asking my friend and fellow fantasy fanatic Mere for an audiobook recommendation, which she enthusiastically delivered: "Deborah Harkness's *A Discovery of Witches*! You'll love it." Thus began my favorite fantasy love affair and my introduction to alchemy.

The entire literary series revolves around alchemy, from an enchanted alchemical manuscript to multiple characters who practice the mystical art. I was totally hooked. After inhaling the book over the course of a few very late nights, I wanted to learn more about this bizarre, esoteric art form known as alchemy.

What first drew me to alchemy was its balancing act between magic and science, between the unknowable and the knowable. Alchemy marries physical, practical pursuits (such as transforming lead into gold) with the spiritual and mental pursuits of self-transformation. This marriage between the physical and metaphysical can be misinterpreted as a sort of witchcraft, but for alchemists, it's just how they saw the world. They understood that they could change themselves and the world around them through the alchemical principles of transformation. It's an assumption not all that different from the principles of modern medicine and science today.

Alchemists were the mystics of their time, working to transform their base souls and minds into their highest, divine form. Alchemists held space for the unknown, creating a way to interpret and understand the world around them. Alchemists essentially created their own religion.

Alchemy, as with many traditions in history, never truly disappeared. Rather, it evolved. Many modern sciences have alchemy entangled in their origin stories. From chemistry and quantum physics to psychology and literature, alchemy and its principles have been woven into the fabric of today's society.

The book you hold in your hands is a mix of alchemy's history, its guiding principles, fun facts, historical profiles, and unique experiments and exercises. It's my hope that this book will be a digestible, fun journey through alchemy, one that demystifies the cryptic concepts and symbols behind this ancient art form. In *Part I: The Foundations of Alchemy*, we'll journey into alchemy's basics, including the role of the elements and a primer about what the Great Work is. In *Part II: Alchemy in All Things Great and Small,* we will consider the cosmos and beyond, examining all the ways alchemy endures today. And through thought experiments and safe at-home exercises, you'll become a budding alchemist in your own right!

Studying alchemy, and now writing about it, has made me all the more curious about our world and our place in it. When I cook, I can't help but think about the stages of transformation my food undergoes, from being plucked from the soil, transformed in my sauté pan, to ending up on my dinner plate. When I think about my place in this wonderful world of ours, I think of the alchemists who believed that all religions stemmed from the same source. The alchemists believed that our great work in life is to better ourselves and the world around us. Whether this is the first you've heard of alchemy or you're already knee-deep in the alchemical cauldron, studying alchemy will make you a more inquisitive, thoughtful, and questioning human being.

Welcome to the adventure!

PART I

THE FOUNDATIONS OF ALCHEMY

○ In this first section, we'll be diving into Alchemy 101,

◐ from the nitty-gritty of defining it and discussing where

● it came from to untangling the three most prominent

forms of alchemy (Physical, Mental, and Spiritual).
We'll take a look at the importance of each element and
how those elements work together to create alchemical
concepts such as First Matter, the Philosopher's Stone, and
the Great Work. Then we'll bring together what we've
learned and explore the three phases of the Great Work.
Congratulations, dear apprentice, on embarking upon the
first step of your journey!

CHAPTER 1

What Is Alchemy?

In chapter 1, we'll construct and explore the backbone of what alchemy is all about. We'll define alchemy, get into its ancient Egyptian roots, and discuss the three most important facets of alchemy: Physical (the actual performing of experiments), Spiritual (the mystical dimension of alchemy), and Mental (how the notion of alchemical self-transformation was adopted by psychologists to change mental habits in a practical way). Lastly, we'll launch into one of the most important foundational principles: the mysterious Seven Stages of transformation.

The Beginnings of Alchemy

S O, WHAT IS ALCHEMY, ANYHOW? *Alchemy is the art of transformation.* That's it! But read on, for that's only the beginning.

The goal of alchemy is transformation for the better (be that actual gold or a golden spirit). Transforming base metals into their essence (lead into gold, for instance) is both an actual, alchemical experiment and a roadmap for transforming the spirit or mind. Alchemists work to transform all things into their highest form, and thus change the course of that thing's life or existence. This is what alchemy is all about—uncovering the essence of everything.

The word "alchemy" (and "chemistry" for that matter) comes from the Egyptian word *khem*, which refers to the natural process of transformation along the banks of the Nile River. Every year, the Nile would flood depositing *khem*, the fertile black soil that was integral for supporting ancient Egyptian agriculture. The earliest books on alchemy appeared around 2,000 years ago in Egypt, China, Mesopotamia, and India.

By 300 CE, the basic principles of alchemy were well established, and they influenced everything from Aristotle's philosophy to Chinese Taoism. Alchemy's huge breadth of influence was largely thanks to the Egyptian library at Alexandria, which housed all the most important alchemical texts and became a mecca for alchemists and scholars of the ancient world. Those texts risked being lost to the world if it weren't for the Arabs who, after taking control of Alexandria along with the rest of Egypt, translated and expanded upon the work of the Egyptian and Greek alchemists before them. Arab alchemists made many important alchemical discoveries, like the concept of alchemical Sulfur and Mercury.

In the early Middle Ages, Arab culture came into contact with Europe in Spain and southern Italy, allowing for the exchange of Arab ideas and innovations, including alchemy. Arab alchemical texts were translated into Latin, and the study of alchemy quickly spread throughout all of medieval Europe. The Church wasn't too keen on this new alchemical fascination. What to alchemists were soul-transforming experiments seemed to the Church a little too much like magic. Alchemists did their

Meet

Thoth

According to Egyptian legend, the god Thoth, often depicted as a man with the head of an ibis and carrying a tablet, shared alchemy's secrets with the ancient Egyptians. The tablet indicated one of the greatest gifts Thoth bestowed upon Egypt: the knowledge of writing. In fact, the role of scribes was so mysterious and important to ancient Egyptians that many of the group were believed to be sorcerers.

Writing's association with magic transformed Thoth into the god of wisdom and sorcery. Ancient Egyptians believed that Thoth initiated the creation of the world and existed everywhere simultaneously. Considered the father of many disciplines—mathematics, agriculture, medicine, religion, and magic—along with alchemy, Thoth is said to have written one of the seminal alchemical texts, *The Emerald Tablet*. The text encompassed Thoth's esoteric teachings on alchemy, and would inspire figures such as Isaac Newton and Robert Bacon.

The Greeks eventually came to associate Thoth with their messenger god, Hermes. Medieval alchemists would later call him Hermes Trismegistus, or "thrice great Hermes," alluding to how true alchemical transformation occurs on three levels of reality: Physical, Spiritual, and Mental.

best to hide and code their experiments in Christian language and symbols, but it wasn't always enough to convince the Church. Alchemists, even today, are often misrepresented as kooky, Merlin-like sorcerers. It's an association that bears some truth, though, since so much of alchemy dances between the unknown and the known, the metaphysical and physical.

By 1595, physical (experiment-based) alchemy began to be separated from more ephemeral mental and spiritual alchemy, which worked to transform the mind and spiritual self. Throughout the 17th century, chemistry began to emerge, and by the 18th century, chemistry had altogether supplanted alchemy. Alchemy was pushed to the fringes, relegated to being the pseudoscience that created chemistry rather than a complex philosophical system that had been practiced for millennia.

It's largely thanks to the psychologist Carl Jung that the metaphysical dimension of alchemy returned to prominence in the 20th century. The alchemists' understanding of mental transformation inspired Jung's own understanding of how to treat his patients. Today, Jungian psychology has given rise to the modern conception of Mental Alchemy.

In the following sections, I'll dive into the three dominant forms of alchemy today: mental, spiritual, and physical, to frame each one in its own separate context.

The Different Facets of Alchemy

When you think of an alchemist, you probably imagine a bearded old man in a castle dungeon surrounded by bubbling potions and mystical powders, working day and night to turn lead into gold. Turning lead into gold was certainly a piece of the alchemical puzzle, and a few legendary alchemists are even believed to have successfully created gold, but there's a lot more to alchemy. Alchemists from around the world conducted all sorts of outlandish experiments. Chinese alchemists, for instance, invented a little-known exploding powder called *huoyao,* or gunpowder.

Luckily for those of us who aren't looking to make explosives in our kitchens, alchemy isn't just pyrotechnics. Alchemical transformations (or transmutations) can either be physical (such as our bearded friend turning lead into gold) or metaphysical (concerning the soul or mind). Transformations are happening around us all the time. Merely acknowledging the ubiquity of transformation, alchemists believed, allows one to start to see the essence of the universe, what alchemists called the "One Mind."

Physical (or exoteric) Alchemy is based on the transformation of actual substances using the elements (air, fire, water, and earth). Alchemists devised all sorts of experiments, from creating a golden tree in a test tube (the Philosopher's Tree) to burning lead-based powders to create a golden fire (the Black Dragon). Scratch beneath the surface, and changing lead into gold is only the beginning.

Alchemists were equally committed to transforming themselves, since it was believed that only an alchemist with a pure soul could successfully transmute base metals into higher metals.

In esoteric or Spiritual Alchemy, the same steps used to turn lead into gold were used to transform "leaden," impure souls into enlightened, "golden" souls. Unlike typical religious study or prayer, spiritual alchemy is all about refining the baser parts of

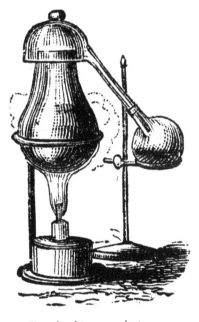

The *alembic*, an enduring tool of physical alchemy

yourself (such as your fears, doubts, and self-hatred) to reveal your truest, enlightened self. It's like achieving nirvana or becoming awakened.

While spiritual alchemy is about transforming your soul, Mental Alchemy is about transforming your mind. Studying mental alchemy can help you break free from familiar mental ruts, like looking at your phone right when you wake up in the morning. In mental alchemy, you take

Alchemy Applied

Make Your Own Edible Lavender Tincture

Use this experiment to both craft an edible tincture tinged with lavender essence and to embrace one of the most important tenets of alchemy: the enduring reality of physical transformation.

INGREDIENTS

4 ounces lavender flowers (or 2 ounces dried), by weight

16 ounces 100-proof vodka, brandy, or rum (or food-grade vegetable glycerin)

TOOLS

Food scale

Quart-size airtight glass container

Fine-mesh sieve or coffee filter

Food processor or blender (optional)

A sunny windowsill

1. Measure out the lavender with a scale (about a tennis ball-sized amount) and, using a food processor, blender, or knife, chop the lavender as small as you can.

2. Put the lavender into the glass container. If you want to add alchemical potency to your tincture, time Step 3 to take place during the full moon.

3. Pour the alcohol or vegetable glycerin in until it covers the herbs by two inches. Incorporate some mental alchemy by writing down something you want to purify or let go of within your own life on a small piece of paper. Put this in the liquid. (Remember though that if you want a transformation to work, you have to follow through with Spiritual and Mental Alchemy, too.)

4. Close the lid and shake. Place the container near a sunny windowsill.

5. Shake the contents once or twice a day for two to six weeks. Notice how the lavender breaks down, transforming into an altogether new substance.

6. Once the desired time has passed, strain the contents of the jar. If you combined the contents in step 2 at the full moon, wait for the following full moon to do this step, adding potency to your tincture.

7. Using a fine-mesh sieve or coffee filter, strain the tincture again.

8. Observe the black matter left behind. Reflect on what the lavender flowers used to look like. If you wrote something you wanted to release, reflect on how that process has evolved.

9. Store the tincture in a dark glass container or a clear-glass container in a cool, dark place. Be sure to label the container with date and contents.

Uses: Alcohol tinctures don't really go bad, but if you've used vegetable glycerin, your tincture is best used within two to three years. Your tincture is 100 percent edible, so add to any and all cooking. Put a few drops in your water bottle or rub onto your temples to aid in relieving headaches, anxiety, or to help induce a peaceful and relaxed sleep.

small, actionable steps toward changing your mind into a friendly, welcoming place full of kind and understanding thoughts.

In the next three sections, I'll dive further into these three forms of alchemy, underscoring how you can implement these different facets into your life right now.

Physical Alchemy

Physical Alchemy is all about the practical, in-the-laboratory elements of alchemy. One of the most important experiments in physical alchemy is the transformation of baser metals into higher metals.

In alchemy, the transformation of any material could be accomplished through the successful completion of the Seven Stages of transformation. For now, all you need to know is that the goal of these stages is to refine any material to its purest state.

This work to purify matter is known as the Great Work, or Magnum Opus, and it could ultimately result in creating the Philosopher's Stone. According to lore, the Philosopher's Stone is a physical substance capable of transforming anything into its highest form. To create the Philosopher's Stone, an alchemist needs to unify all the opposing elements (air, fire, water, and earth). I'll delve deeper into the elements in chapter 2, but for the time being just know that alchemy is all about unifying opposites such as these.

Now, you might be thinking that physical alchemy has all but been replaced by chemistry. While it is true that physical alchemy eventually gave rise to modern chemistry, chemistry still owes a huge debt to alchemy. Early alchemists developed some of the earliest-known laboratory equipment, some of which chemists still use today.

Around 200 CE, Maria Prophetissa (also known as "Mary the Jewess") invented a host of different alchemical equipment, including the *tribikos*. The *tribikos* is a double-walled container and type of alembic that aids in the collection and distillation of heated substances. Today, modern versions of the *tribikos* are still used in chemistry labs all over the world.

Beyond what alchemy has given chemistry, some academics continue to practice physical alchemy, like the history and science professor Lawrence Principe. Tucked away in a small university laboratory, Principe

Taming the Alchemical Dragon:

A Meditation

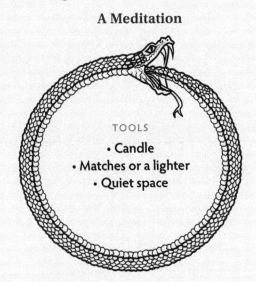

TOOLS

- Candle
- Matches or a lighter
- Quiet space

FIND a quiet place where you won't be disturbed. Sit in a comfortable position that allows you to have a straight spine, as in a chair with your feet on the floor and back supported. Take a few deep breaths in through your nose and out through your mouth. Do this until you feel your mind and body begin to settle. Notice your thoughts, but allow them to drift away like fallen leaves on a stream.

PLACE the candle in front of you. Light the candle to symbolize the active, energetic work you're about to undertake with the Alchemical Dragon. Close your eyes or rest your gaze on the flame.

BEGIN to breathe by forcing the air out on an active exhale and allowing air to fill the vacuum in a passive inhale. Time one breath cycle to about one second. (This breathing technique is known in kundalini yoga as "dragon's breath" or "breath of fire.") Do this for a few minutes.

RETURN to your normal breathing pattern. Close your eyes and feel your body fill with the energy of the Alchemical Dragon. Take a moment to set an intention that tackles personal or cultural chaotic energy (like finishing that work assignment or volunteering for a political campaign).

BLOW out the candle.

Alchemy Applied

Using Mental Alchemy to Transform Inadequacy into Power

FIND a quiet, comfortable space where you won't be disturbed.

CLOSE your eyes and take some deep, centering breaths.

THINK back to a recent moment when you felt inadequate, such as your boss giving you a hard time at work or missing a deadline to apply to something you were excited about. Where were you? What did it feel like? Replay the moment as though you're watching a scene from a movie.

SEND strength and power to this former, hurting version of yourself. Give yourself a hug or offer yourself some imaginary chocolate. What would've made you feel better in that moment? Do it now in your imagination.

IMAGINE a shimmering aura of pure white light surrounding you, burning away those feelings of inadequacy. See your aura glow brighter as it consumes any and all negativity.

SEE the radiant, beautiful person you are shining bright. Breathe this image in.

DISAPPOINTMENTS happen, but know they don't define you. All of this is part of life. These experiences don't define you.

OPEN your eyes and know you are enough.

tries to decode experiments from alchemists' strange symbols and cryptic writings to better understand the alchemists of centuries past.

There's also the International Alchemy Guild (IAG), which was founded in 1998 by the author and modern-day alchemist Dennis William Hauck. The IAG was founded to educate and support the work of those interested in physical alchemy today. According to the IAG, there are more licensed alchemists now than ever before.

But even if you aren't ready to hop into an accredited alchemist-training program, physical alchemy still has a lot to offer. Our bodies and lives are full of physical transformations. Just look at an old photograph and notice how you've aged. Or watch spinach turn a vibrant green in the sauté pan. Physical alchemy is all around us in these everyday transformations. Taking the time to acknowledge these transformations is the easiest way to understand a basic tenet of alchemy—transformation is everywhere. When we acknowledge that truth, it helps connect us to the energy of the universe, or the "One Mind" as alchemists put it.

Spiritual Alchemy

In alchemy, a transformation can be sustained only if it occurs on all levels of reality: physical, spiritual, and mental. So, now that you have a firm grasp on what physical alchemy is all about, let's explore **Spiritual Alchemy**.

Spiritual alchemy is rooted in the transformation of the spirit and soul. It's important to note that, for alchemists, spirit and soul are *not* synonymous. In alchemy, one's spirit is constantly striving toward betterment, and it is associated with the all-important symbol of the Red King. One's soul seeks contentment in the moment, and is associated with the equally important White Queen. Just as opposing elemental forces must be combined in physical alchemy, the same is true in spiritual alchemy. The opposing forces of the soul and spirit must be joined together in order to transform into our highest, "golden" self. The union of the Red King and White Queen is the most pivotal stage of alchemical transformation. Their union is known as the Sacred Marriage (more on that in chapter 3).

Practicing physical alchemy in the laboratory goes along with spiritual alchemy, for when alchemists work to transform lead into gold, they also work to transform their spiritual selves. In the same way that yoga is a physical practice to transform the spirit, so is alchemy.

Spiritual alchemy is different from a request made in prayer, the inner silence cultivated in meditation, or other forms of religious practice. In alchemy, an individual's willpower or "fire" drives spiritual transformation. You are the only person who can change yourself; you have the alchemical tools to do so, but it's up to you to master and implement them.

Transforming one's immortal essence into its highest form is grueling work aligned with the symbol of the dragon in both Eastern and Western alchemy. In physical alchemy, the **Alchemical Dragon** is associated with a mysterious, indefinable substance known as Philosophical Mercury. Philosophical Mercury is different from your run-of-the mill mercury, or quicksilver. Physical Alchemy is the raw energy of the world. A true transformation of any substance (be it lead or our spiritual selves) cannot occur without the Alchemical Dragon; that is, without harnessing the world's energy.

In spiritual alchemy, working with the Alchemical Dragon is all about transforming chaotic energy, a process that occurs on a personal level and on a greater cultural level. One way to transform chaotic energy on a personal level is by arriving 10 minutes early to everything rather than always running late. On a cultural level, the transformation of chaotic energy might resemble tackling greater cultural issues, such as war or poverty. Effective change usually stems from the personal. For instance, to tackle the cultural chaos of poverty at the personal level, you could start working at a soup kitchen once a week. After becoming aware of the chaos in our lives, our only choice is accepting it and working with that chaos toward something better. It is not a matter of conquering the chaos of the Alchemical Dragon, but of learning to be still within that chaos and doing what we can to harness that chaotic energy. Don't let the enormity

Alchemy Applied

Working With Your Alchemical Dragon:

A Journal Exercise

MATERIALS

Pen or Pencil • Journal

START by becoming aware of any moments throughout the day, week, or month when your world felt chaotic. First, just identify the moment. Making a mental note, "things feel a little chaotic right now." Try to do this without judgment.

FIND a quiet, safe place where you can reflect and write, somewhere where you won't be disturbed.

LIST all the chaotic moments you remember from your past day, week, or month. Examine your list. Do you see any similarities? Are you always worried about running late? Notice what sort of circumstances lead to a feeling of chaos. Do things always feel chaotic when you don't get enough sleep? When you get too much sleep? After you drink alcohol?

CREATE one small, actionable step you can take in the next week to help minimize that chaos. Like going to bed at the same time every night. Or putting your phone away once you get into bed. Enjoying sparkling water instead of a cocktail.

AFTER a week, reflect about what it was like to implement that one step. Did it minimize the chaos a bit? Don't be too hard on yourself if you slip back into old patterns. The point is to become aware and begin to transition. Instead of beating yourself up, try to just do better tomorrow.

It takes about month for a habit to stick. So, if your actionable step helps minimize the chaos in your life, keep it up! If it adds to the chaos, choose a different step to implement.

of cultural chaos stop you from doing anything as an individual—you have the power to make a difference.

The Alchemical Dragon is often depicted as the **Ouroboros**, an ancient symbol of a dragon or serpent devouring its own tail. For alchemists, the Ouroboros is a symbolic representation of how energy is neither created nor destroyed, only transformed. Alchemists believe that each of us has the power to transform our spiritual selves; it's merely a matter of doing the work.

Mental Alchemy

In order for a transformation to be lasting, alchemists believed, change had to also occur in the mind of the individual. This is known as **Mental Alchemy**. This third form of alchemy is about transforming your identity, and ultimately realizing that the identity (or ego) is unknowable.

Mental alchemy is deeply linked with the Swiss psychoanalyst Carl Jung, who found alchemy to be a sort of master key to unlocking the human subconscious, using it to transform the minds of his patients. Jung credited alchemy for his understanding of how the Unconscious transforms and evolves over a lifetime. In fact, Jung amassed one of the largest libraries of original alchemical texts in Europe.

The core work in mental alchemy is to break down that which has become rigid in our identities, and any rigid form is known as a **Salt**. In physical alchemy, a Salt is a solid. In mental alchemy, a Salt is the limiting understanding of who we are. Consider how all little kids are artists, with no qualms about singing or showing off a piece of art they made. But as we get older, we're told to focus on more "useful" or "profitable" endeavors. How many people do you know would balk at the idea of drawing a picture or getting onstage? Any time you hear yourself or others say, "Oh, no, I couldn't possibly do that," it is indicative of a Salt, of some limiting belief about one's identity.

In order to break down these personality Salts, one must tap back into the **First Matter** (or Prima Materia) of the universe. I'll go into far more detail on First Matter in chapter 2, but to briefly define it: First Matter is the chaotic, raw, Dragon energy of the world and the essence of all things.

It's similar to the Hindu concept of *Brahman* or physics's string theory. In Hinduism, *Brahman* is the eternal energy that is the source of all things. In quantum physics, string theory examines how the most basic particles of matter interact.

But how do we harness the concept of First Matter to transform the Salt in our personalities? It's simple on a rudimentary level: seek out new experiences. Start journaling. Go see a movie. Skydive. Go on a date. Do something scary. Whenever you feel yourself about to say, "No, I can't do that," do it anyway.

Let's consider how going to a movie can be mental alchemy. Have you ever seen a movie that completely gutted you and left you unable to form a coherent sentence afterwards? That feeling is your identity or Salts fracturing. It's in that raw, open state that you can access First Matter and feel the interconnectedness of all things. As you have more and more of these identity-fracturing experiences, you'll become comfortable with the fact that our identities are not fixed things and that we all spring from the same source, known to alchemists as First Matter.

Other Forms of Alchemy

Even though physical, spiritual, and mental alchemy make up the three fundamental types of alchemy, there are other types out there.

First, let's look at **Artistic Alchemy**. Art, primarily the visual arts, has been intertwined with alchemy since alchemy's beginning. Dyes, paints, jewelry making, sculpting, and perfume all owe a big debt to alchemists. Plenty of contemporary artists view themselves as modern alchemists, making art that's meant to transform over time.

The contemporary artist Faith Sponsler creates work that often undergoes a chemical reaction to reveal something new. Her iron-soaked linoleum cut prints, for instance, turn a very dark color after being soaked in green tea.

The chemical transformation necessary to process film has brought alchemy into photography and moviemaking. The photographer Matthew Cetta embraced the connections between photography and alchemy in his series *Photogenic Alchemy*, using everything from Ambien to Drano

Breaking Down Your Salts:

A Journal Exercise

MATERIALS

Pen or Pencil • Journal

FIND a cozy, quiet spot where you can reflect without judgment.

THINK about some dares that would push you to your edge, like skydiving or asking a friend to set you up on a date. Write a few of these examples down in your journal. What would you do if you know it'd go over well? Would you give the cute bassist your number if you knew they'd call? Would you take the skydiving leap if you knew it would change your life?

CIRCLE one dare, and do it this week! Something that scares you, that pushes you to your edge. Perhaps even convince a friend to do it with you! That way you hold yourself accountable.

AFTER you've completed your dare, reflect upon how it went. How did you feel? Try to remove yourself from a specific, desired outcome. For instance, think about how it felt to give a stranger your number, and not about whether they called or not.

ONCE you've rewarded yourself with something indulgent (a piece of dark chocolate perhaps?), choose another dare! It's important to give yourself a moment to reflect and recharge, but it's equally important to get back out there and do something else that scares you.

LOOK at you breaking down your Salts!

as mediums to develop film. We'll delve deeper into the connections between art and alchemy in chapter 5, but suffice it to say—there's a lot!

Spiritual and mental alchemy have inspired filmmakers and storytellers at large to create nuanced stories about personal and spiritual transformation. Alchemy inspired Joseph Campbell's concept of the hero's journey, which in turn inspired the sci-fi franchise *Star Wars* (more on that in chapter 5).

Social Alchemy is rooted in the transformation of relationships. It encompasses both personal relationship transformation (between friends or lovers) and societal transformation (such as ending poverty or slavery). The term itself gained traction in the last century, and it has become intertwined with many of the social movements of the 20th century.

In the vein of mental alchemy, a different but related form is **Psychological Alchemy**. Though both mental and psychological alchemy are indebted to Carl Jung, psychological alchemy is more anchored in how the principles of alchemy continue to influence psychology. Alchemical principles can be seen in everything from personality tests to archetypes, which are both rooted in Jung's theories of the mind and drawn from alchemy.

It's important to note that our earlier alchemist friends wouldn't have seen the same minute distinctions between the different forms as we do today. For them, any form of transformation is a form of alchemy, because all transformations spring forth from First Matter. Alchemy is only about returning to the highest, "golden" state embodied in First Matter. For alchemists, it doesn't matter if this transformation is on a therapist's couch, in an artist's studio, or in society at large; it's all part of the same thing.

The Seven Stages of Alchemy

THE ALCHEMISTS IDENTIFIED **Seven Stages of Alchemy** necessary for any transformation. Regardless of if a transformation is physical, spiritual or mental, it involves passing through all of these seven stages. Alchemists were a very secretive bunch and often wrote about the Seven Stages using esoteric symbols and metaphors. This was especially prevalent during the 16th century, when alchemists could be burned at the stake as witches and heretics. While getting burned at the stake is certainly a form of transformation, it was not exactly the kind alchemists were going for.

Collectively, the Seven Stages make up the **Great Work**, or Magnum Opus, which, when followed properly, results in the purification and refinement of any material into its highest form. If the Seven Stages are successful, an alchemist can achieve the Philosopher's Stone, the Holy Grail that can transform anything into its supreme, "golden" form.

Alchemists divide the Seven Stages into three phases: the **Blackening**, or *Nigredo*, (pronounced *nee-GRAY-doe*); the **Whitening**, or *Albedo* (*al-BAY-doe*); and the **Reddening**, or *Rubedo* (*ruh-BAY-doe*). I'll explain these three phases in more detail in chapter 3. For now, we'll focus on grasping what the Seven Stages are all about.

STAGE 1 — The Calcination Stage of *Nigredo*

In physical alchemy, **Calcination** entails burning a substance over a flame or with a "liquid fire," such as an acid or corrosive chemical, until the substance is reduced to ashes. The word itself means "reduced to bone by burning."

In mental and spiritual alchemy, Calcination happens whether we want it to or not. Calcination occurs whenever life knocks us down—everything from failing your driver's test to your first breakup. It's easy to let these disappointments get you down. What's harder is to rise up from the ashes, as we'll see in later stages.

STAGE

2

The Dissolution Stage of *Nigredo*

In physical alchemy, **Dissolution** (sometimes just called Solution) takes the ashes produced in Calcination and dissolves them in a liquid solvent. This process is where we get the word "elixir," which comes from the Arabic *al-iksir,* "from the ashes."

In mental and spiritual alchemy, Dissolution refers to breaking down all the Salts, or assumptions that have snuck into our unconscious. In Dissolution, one must look at their "shadow," our dark side, and interrogate the unconscious messages that have unknowingly entered our minds, whether they are simple, such as problematically biased news, or a bit more complex.

STAGE

3

The Separation Stage of *Albedo*

In physical alchemy, **Separation** discards the waste from Dissolution and Calcination to retrieve the matter's essential parts. To accomplish separation, the liquid of Dissolution is usually passed through a filter or porous paper.

In mental and spiritual alchemy, Separation is about looking objectively at the parts of your personality and spiritual self and discarding what no longer serves you. In doing so, you recognize your true self, devoid of ego or the superfluous aspects of your personality.

STAGE

4

The Conjunction Stage of *Albedo*

In physical alchemy, **Conjunction** takes the purified matter from Separation and creates an altogether new substance. Alchemists called this new substance "the child of the Conjunction." Failing to create a new substance means that the matter extracted from Separation is contaminated and the alchemist's experiment has failed.

In mental and spiritual alchemy, Conjunction combines the opposing parts of the self to create a new personality or spiritual self. In mental alchemy, this is about joining your conscious and unconscious minds. In spiritual alchemy, this is about combining your spirit and soul. This is also where the Sacred Marriage is consummated, creating the fetus of the child of Conjunction (also known as the newly created substance).

STAGE

5

The Fermentation Stage of *Rubedo*

In physical alchemy, **Fermentation** is where the "child" from Conjunction is matured with fermenting bacteria over a low, controlled heat (unlike the direct flames of Calcination). Fermentation is where the "fetus" of Conjunction slowly grows as the introduction of bacteria animates the matter to take on a new form.

In spiritual and mental alchemy, Fermentation marks a moment when new life is brought into the mind and spiritual self. This can take the form of delving into a new religious practice, meditation, or exercising regularly. Fermentation is anything that adds an external spark to your life. It's best if this isn't reliant on another person and is more self-contained. It's more reliable to fall in love with yourself, after all, than with a new lover or friend.

STAGE

6

The Distillation Stage of *Rubedo*

In physical alchemy, **Distillation** purifies the now-fermented substance to its essence through evaporation or cohobation (repeatedly purifying a substance in liquid).

In spiritual or mental alchemy, Distillation requires you to repeatedly open up space to have new insights, and then work to purify yourself based upon those insights. Therapy is a great example of distillation. Therapists help their clients make breakthroughs and then reintegrate those breakthroughs into their minds and spiritual selves.

STAGE

7

The Coagulation Stage of *Rubedo*

In physical alchemy, **Coagulation** is the final stage of alchemical transformation, where the essence refined in Distillation is solidified. It's when the child of Conjunction is born and all this work takes form both physically and metaphysically. It's the moment when the body becomes metaphysical and the spirit and mind take on a corporeal form.

In spiritual and mental alchemy, Coagulation is the physical manifestation of the spiritual body and mind, much like an aura of light surrounding your body. It's in this stage of transformation that all the elements and levels of reality (physical, spiritual, and mental) become one.

Into THE Elements

Look at you! You've passed Alchemy 101. Here are some key takeaways:

- Alchemy is the art of transformation.

- Alchemy originated in ancient Egypt about 2,000 years ago.

- Alchemists believed there are three main levels of reality—physical, mental, and spiritual—and a transformation had to occur on all these levels to be effective.

- Physical alchemy is the practical, in-the-laboratory component of alchemy.

- Spiritual alchemy works to transform the soul and spirit.

- Mental alchemy works to transform the mind.

- There are Seven Stages of an alchemical transformation.

In the next chapter, let's dive deeper into how the four elements (air, fire, water, and earth) influence these Seven Stages and alchemy as a whole.

CHAPTER 2

Alchemy and ̲T̲H̲E̲ Elements

Early philosophers believed that the four elements of air, fire, water, and earth made up the basic building blocks of the world. In alchemy, the elements are created through raw energy known as First Matter, the chaotic, purest energy present in all things. When thinking alchemically, combining all the elements is the only path to true transformation. Without the elements, alchemical transformation is impossible.

FIRE

HOT · DRY

AIR · EARTH

WET · COLD

WATER

ᴛʜᴇ Four Elements

ɴ ᴀʟᴄʜᴇᴍʏ, the elements are manifestations of spiritual essence, of **First Matter**, or Prima Materia. But where First Matter is chaotic and unstructured, the elements are decidedly more organized.

The pre-Socratic philosophers of ancient Greece were among the first to really look to the organization of the natural world independent from myths. Thales first proposed the element water as nature's basic building block in the sixth century BCE. Fifty years later, Anaximenes added air. Another 50 years after that, Xenophanes added earth. In the fifth century BCE, Heraclitus brought fire into the mix. Empedocles soon after unified his predecessors' theories into the four elements: the "eternal elements." He believed change occurred through the combining or rearranging of elements. Plato later described the elements as "idea-forms," providing form to all things.

Aristotle believed that the elements each manifested two of four qualities (hot, dry, wet, and cold), and he added the fifth element, Ether, to the mix. Ether, as Aristotle put forth, is the building block of the heavens or the divine realm. In alchemy, this fifth element is referred to as **Quintessence**, the spark of some higher power. The Quintessence is a way of holding space for what will always be unknown, and yet it was the alchemists' task to capture this unknowable essence in their experiments. For our purposes, though, we will be focusing on the four elements of our world.

The elements instigate all transformations in physical, spiritual, and mental alchemy. In physical alchemy, the elements are integral to each of the Seven Stages. In spiritual and mental alchemy, the elements represent opposing aspects of the spiritual self and mind that must be unified in a successful transformation. All the elements are associated with purification and are used to purify the mind, spirit, and physical substances in alchemy.

Water

When Thales first proposed water as an element, he believed it to be the basic building block of the world. In fact, creation myths from across the globe tell stories of the primordial waters of the world. Alchemists believed that their work was a microcosm of God's creation of the world. With the rise of Christianity in medieval Europe, medieval alchemists would relate their alchemical work to the Genesis passage in which God moves on the face of the waters before creating the world.

Water plays an important role in Dissolution and Distillation, too. In both of these stages, a liquid solvent is introduced to purify the matter undergoing transformation. In essence, the element of water "baptizes" the material. In Dissolution, this is a baptism of death, of ego, a letting go of the self. In Distillation, this is the baptism of new life as the child of Conjunction is "born."

In spiritual and mental alchemy, the qualities of water are used to purify the mind or spiritual self. This can take the form of a long bath, swimming in the ocean, or taking a moment to contemplate the rain and allowing yourself to really feel cleansed in the process. Introducing

Elementally, Dear Alchemist

All alchemists have a close relationship with the elements, but for the Alexandrian alchemists Kleopatra and Hypatia (shown at center), and the Renaissance figure Paracelsus, it was a marriage that lasted a lifetime.

A contemporary of Maria Prophetissa, Kleopatra invented the alembic or stillhead, allowing alchemists to purify substances during Distillation. Only fragments of Kleopatra's writing still exist, but the little we do have talks of the importance of the elements, especially water.

Much of Hypatia's (370–415 CE) writings have also been lost, but we know that she improved upon Kleopatra's alembic and created her own contraptions to help in Distillation. She invented a device to measure water levels as well as a graduated hydroscope, or hydrometer, which measures a liquid's gravity.

The daughter of a mathematician and astronomer, Hypatia traveled extensively before becoming University of Alexandria's chair of mathematics and philosophy. She was a favorite professor, and government officials often called upon her for guidance, but she met a horrible end. A pagan, Hypatia was killed by a mob of Christian monks who flayed and quartered her.

Many contemporary scholars view her death as the end of an age of innovation, a testament to Hypatia's brilliance.

During the Renaissance, the alchemist Paracelsus used the elements to transform the field of medicine. While wandering with Romani across Europe, he learned medical folklore from midwives. To him, nature was the true pharmacy. One had only to study her and her elements to find effective cures. Despite his vagabond streak, Paracelsus developed an early form of morphine, *laudanum*, and processes for making medicines that are still used.

water to the spirit and mind means gently washing away assumptions or hang-ups.

The Greek physician Hippocrates (460–370 BCE), considered the father of modern medicine, believed that the elements also existed within our bodies, identifying four bodily "humors." He identified water with phlegm, the clear fluids of the body. A person with phlegm is emotional, flexible, introverted, and calm. Aristotle also identified such people with the element of water, which he associated with the qualities cold and wet. The psychoanalyst Carl Jung perpetuated Hippocrates's and Aristotle's notions of the elements in his development of personality archetypes.

As with all things in alchemy, water must be joined with the other three opposing elements in order for the final stage of Coagulation to be successful.

Fire

In alchemy, fire is considered the most important element, because it's always changing. As Heraclitus understood it, fire manifests the old adage, "The only constant is change." Alchemists identified four different kinds of fire. The first, **Elementary Fire**, is the common fire we're all familiar with: the fire of candles, stovetops, and campfires. The second, **Celestial Fire**, is the brilliant, white fire of the divine will: "God's fire." The third, **Central Fire**, is the fire between Celestial Fire and Elementary Fire: the fire of creation. The fourth and final fire, **Secret Fire**, is the precise fire of alchemical experiments (both the inner experiments of spiritual and mental alchemy and the outer experiments of physical alchemy). Secret Fire is the fire of life, the Quintessence, the inner spark we've spoken about that makes every transformation possible.

Fire is associated with many of the Seven Stages, particularly Calcination and Fermentation. As the first stage, Calcination initiates all alchemical transformations and uses fire to reduce a substance to ashes, like when obstacles apply "heat" to our lives. In Fermentation, fire is applied in a steady manner to coax the substance to take on a new form.

This is the controlled heat of delving into oneself (such as through journaling, therapy, or meditation) to find our truest selves.

In mental and spiritual alchemy, fire is the sought and unsought events in our lives that change us. The moments of dramatic change—such as a loved one passing or a natural disaster, as well as the controlled change that comes from soul-searching in therapy or reading self-help books—all represent fire in our lives.

Hippocrates identified fire with the yellow bile of cholesterol, produced as a byproduct of digestion. Hippocrates considered "Choleric" people to be energetic, enthusiastic, motivated, and potentially irritable. Aristotle likewise considered such people to be both hot and dry.

Air

In alchemy, air and earth are seen as elements secondary to water and fire. Air is the "sea of invisible things." Anaximenes championed air as the "breath of life," or *pneuma*, and he considered it the source of all things, not unlike Thales did with water.

Air plays an important role in Distillation as the substance goes through repeated stages of evaporation. In Distillation, the substance is boiled, releasing vapors that are then condensed back into a liquid. Distillation could take months as alchemists continuously boiled and condensed the substance. Due to Distillation's importance as a formational stage of alchemy, it was also a stage where many elements were involved. As noted above, water plays an important role in Distillation as well.

In spiritual and mental alchemy, air, like all the elements, works to purify the mind and spiritual self. The difference is in how. Air evaporates, rising above heavier elements. It's this quality of floating above the other elements that links air with imagination, creativity, and thinking. Driving with the windows open or walking outside to feel the breeze both utilize air to purify your mind and spirit. Moments when your mind or spiritual self seem to float above physical reality (such as when trying to contemplate the vastness of outer space, hearing a powerful sermon, or experimenting with psychedelics) also work with air.

Hippocrates identified air with blood, which we know moves oxygen throughout the body. A person with this "sanguine" humor can be indecisive, optimistic, curious, and intelligent. Aristotle identified air with the qualities of hot and wet, producing a person who can balance the thoughtfulness of air with the empathy of water. Aristotle considered air to be a combination of the wet quality in water and the hot quality of fire.

Earth

Earth is also a secondary element. Xenophanes was the first to incorporate earth (along with water) as one of the basic building blocks of all things. Based upon his study of fossils, Xenophanes assumed that the world oscillates between extreme wetness (water) and extreme dryness (earth), and only when the two are in harmony is life possible.

The earth element is associated with any alchemical transformation that produces a solid or Salt, and it is particularly important in Separation and Conjunction. Separation extracts impure solids (earth) from the essence of the substance. Conjunction creates a new solid (earth) through the combination of fire, water, and air.

In spiritual and mental alchemy, removing impure Salts can purify the mind and spiritual self (as in Separation), eventually creating a new, pure solid (as in Conjunction). Earth has the ability to ground energy and neutralize it. For instance, if you're feeling overwhelmed, lie down on the ground and let that negativity fall away into the Earth.

Hippocrates associated earth with black bile (i.e., bodily waste). People with this "Melancholic" humor are practical, grounded, and self-assured. In Aristotle's terms, such people are cold and dry, because Earth was associated with the cold quality of water and the dry quality of fire.

Understanding First Matter
(Prima Materia)

THERE'S NO WAY TO TALK ABOUT THE ELEMENTS WITHOUT talking about First Matter, that chaotic, universal "Dragon" energy that makes everything possible, and the gray area between what has been created and what hasn't yet been created. It's also matter, the literal "stuff" of the universe, making the definition of First Matter twofold: the energy of the universe and the primordial matter of all things.

This may seem contradictory. How can something both be the energy of the universe and the matter that makes up the universe? Well, for alchemists, all matter carries energy.

Pre-Socratic philosophers looked to different elements as the basic matter of the universe, but it's not really until the pre-Socratic philosopher Anaxagoras (and to some degree Empedocles) comes along that the concept of First Matter starts to take form. While Empedocles posited that there was a unifying force in the universe, Anaxagoras wrote the earliest reference to First Matter, which he called *nous*. Anaxagoras saw *nous* as omnipresent, omnipotent, and eternal. *Nous*, according to him, was akin to the divine mind presiding over all transformations. But *nous* was also the real matter of the universe, and Anaxagoras called it "the thinnest of things."

All things spring from First Matter. It is the source of the four elements, the Philosopher's Stone, and all metals, along with everything else in the universe. The transformation of lead into gold in alchemy is possible because all metals originate from the same First Matter. It's a theory not all that far from modern chemistry, in which one substance can transform into another through the addition or removal of protons.

First Matter is considered to be the "inner star" of all matter. Medieval alchemists equated First Matter with the soul, and the work of perfecting any matter was the work of perfecting one's soul.

And the ultimate tool of soul perfection was none other than the Philosopher's Stone.

The Flamels and the Philosopher's Stone

Nicolas Flamel (shown at center) was born outside of Paris in 1330 and ran a humble bookstall with his older, wealthier wife, Perenelle.

One night, Nicolas dreamed that an angel gave him an alchemical book containing the recipe to make the legendary Philosopher's Stone. In 1357, a man showed up to sell Nicolas the book from his dream! The mysterious book was full of inde-cipherable, alchemical images and text. The Flamels were only able to make out that it was written in some ancient Hebrew script. Finally, after two years wandering in Spain, Nicolas found an elderly Jewish physician, Maitre Canches, who knew the book to be a legendary cabbalist text. Thanks to Canches, Nicolas and Perenelle were able to decipher the book, and in January 1382, Nicolas wrote that he and Perenelle had made the Philosopher's Stone.

Records indicate the Flamels made generous donations to churches and charities, and that they lived abnormally long lives. Perenelle died in 1397 (though some sources put her death even later, in 1414), and Nicolas died somewhere from 1416 to 1418. According to still other accounts, they may still be alive, living out their retirement in India.

After their (supposed) deaths, their home was sacked in search of the Philosopher's Stone, but it was never found. The Flamels perhaps pulverized the stone into a fine red powder or destroyed it, considering its capabilities too dangerous for humankind.

While there's a lot of lore interwoven into the Flamels' story, we do know Nicolas and Perenelle were alchemists, and that Nicolas wrote about creating the Philosopher's Stone. We know the couple amassed and donated a large fortune, and that Nicolas had alchemical drawings inscribed on his tomb.

Understanding
THE Philosopher's Stone

NOW, THE PHILOSOPHER'S STONE MAY SOUND FAMILIAR, thanks to a little-known series of books written by J. K. Rowling. That's right, the **Philosopher's Stone** (or Sorcerer's Stone, as it was changed to in United States) that features in the first *Harry Potter* book is the same alchemists worked tirelessly to achieve.

Why were the alchemists so keen to create the Philosopher's Stone? Alchemists believed the Stone could change anything base into its highest form. With the help of the Philosopher's Stone, alchemists could achieve their goal of turning lead into gold. While gold was the ultimate, "purest" outcome of an alchemical experiment, the Philosopher's Stone acted essentially like an alchemical hack. It was the active agent that made the transformation possible. According to legend, the stone was red in color, irregular in size, and seen as the ultimate purifying agent. So, in addition to being able to make gold whenever you wanted, the Stone could also purify the human body, enabling its possessor to live forever. Now, who doesn't want that?

For the alchemists, the Philosopher's Stone held dual forms. They believed it to be a real, physical substance, yet also believed it was the knowledge of how to achieve an enlightened mind and spirit. The Stone was the combination of all things: all the elements, all genders, all levels of reality. It was the organization and combination of all opposites, and alchemists were *really* keen on opposites.

When you sift through alchemical manuscripts, you'll find all sorts of opposites. There's the alchemical depiction of the *adrogyne*, an alchemical hermaphrodite that represents, like the Stone, the coming together of opposites. The *adrogyne* was both male and female, both dark-skinned and light, all the opposing elements unified in one substance.

Union of Opposites

M. Maier, Atalanta fugiens, Oppenheim, 1618.

This image depicts the union of opposites so central in alchemy. There's the male and female within a square with a side for each of the four elements within a triangle for the union of body, spirit, and soul.

THE Actual Alchemist

Women in Alchemy

From Isaac Newton to Nicolas Flamel, male alchemists dominate alchemical history. But let's take a moment to honor some of the ladies!

Little is known about the 17th-century French alchemist Marie Meurdrac besides her 1666 alchemical manual, *Charitable and Easy Chemistry for Women*, which (unfortunately) is a theme when it comes to female alchemists. Often, all we know about them is contained in their writings. In her book, Meurdrac tells the reader how she debated publishing the book because she was a woman, ultimately deciding to go ahead with it after concluding that the "mind has no sex."

Her 300-plus-page book discussed alchemical principles, instruments, medicines, animals, and metals, along

Marie Meurdrac
FRANCE
• • • • • •

Isabella Cortese
ITALY
· · · · · ·

with a final section on makeup. The book was very popular during her time, going through multiple editions and translations.

Italian Isabella Cortese is another alchemist we know only through her book published in 1561, *The Secrets of Signora Isabella Cortese*. These popular "books of secrets" were basic alchemy how-to guides.

Cortese writes that it is human to want to understand, perfect, and even outdo nature. Her book contains a variety of alchemical experiments in pursuit of the Great Work and the Philosopher's Stone, as well as some experiments that were female-only (such as healing after childbirth), a common practice in these books of

secrets: women writing these books for other women and about female concerns. Even so, Cortese's book stands out thanks to her extensive incorporation of alchemical secrets.

Thanks to her being the queen of Sweden from age six, we know a good deal about Christina's alchemical practice and how religion, mathematics, alchemy, and philosophy all fascinated her.

She conducted her first known alchemical experiments in 1656, and invited the well-known alchemist Giuseppo Francesco Borri to work with her to try and create the Philosopher's Stone, though it seems that the pair were unsuccessful. Beyond Borri, Christina's court had more than a few alchemists, including followers of Paracelsus.

Queen Christina
SWEDEN
· · · · · ·

According to alchemical lore, Nicolas and Perenelle Flamel success-fully created the Philosopher's Stone with the help of a mythical book. But, alas, the stone was lost to history. Or was it?

Undertaking ᴛʜᴇ Great Work
(Magnum Opus)

NO ONE EXEMPLIFIES THE GREAT WORK (OR MAGNUM OPUS) better than the Flamels. In alchemy, the **Great Work** culminates in making the Philosopher's Stone. The Great Work begins with First Matter, in the form of a base metal. That base metal is then purified and refined to its essence. In physical alchemy, this essence is gold. In mental and spiritual alchemy, this refined essence is the enlightened mind and spiritual self. Creating this pure, highest form (be it gold or the enlightened mind) can only be accomplished through the union of opposites.

The two fundamental opposites of alchemy are **Sulfur** and **Mercury**. In the eighth century, the Arab alchemist Jabir ibn Hayyan (722/723–815 CE) or Geber, as he was known in Medieval Europe, was the first to posit that metals were created depending on their ratio of Sulfur to Mercury and how pure that Sulfur and Mercury were. He also believed that the alignment of planets played an important role in the creation of different metals (more on that in chapter 4).

Jabir believed that gold could only be created through balancing and purifying the Sulfur and Mercury in a base metal. This idea of balance became the premise for how alchemists would attempt to change lead into gold. If you could balance and purify the Sulfur and Mercury of lead, the result would be gold. Jabir spent most of his life trying to create the Philosopher's Stone, setting the precedent for medieval alchemists to follow in his footsteps.

Alchemists believed Mercury to be active, hot, and fiery, and associ-ated Mercury with the symbolic Red King and Sol. Sulfur, on the other hand, was believed to be passive, watery, wet, and was associated with the symbolic White Queen and Luna. The union of these two opposing forces would create the universal solvent (the vaunted Philosopher's Stone). Traditionally, Mercury is associated with the spirit and Sulfur with the soul. Contradicting alchemical texts sometimes switch this association, prescribing Mercury with the contentment of the soul and Sulfur with the striving of the spirit—an inconsistency that goes to show the complex interplay between the two forces.

Alchemists believed that people, too, are made up of Sulfur and Mercury, and that true purification comes from uniting these two opposing forces within us. Many different systems of thought believe in two opposing forces, such as yin and yang in Chinese thought or the South American Andean concept *yanantin*, "complimentary opposites." Alchemists always understood these forces to exist on a gradient. One cannot be wholly Sulfur, and one cannot be wholly Mercury. We all contain elements of both.

The Great Work of mental and spiritual alchemy is to unify these opposites, to balance the Sulfur and Mercury within the personality and spiritual self. In today's world of commoditization, most of us will probably find that we're more Mercurial—more active, striving—and we will need to cultivate more Sulfur and contentment. If that means chilling out with some TV, chill out with some TV. If that means meditating, meditate. Do what works for you. Alchemists were ever the pragmatists.

In chapter 3, we'll delve deeper into the Great Work and its three phases. But before we do, you can cozy up to your own inner divisions between your Sulfur and Mercury sides with some simple journal work.

Are You More Sulfur or Mercury?

A Journal Exercise

MATERIALS

Pen or Pencil • Journal

FIND a quiet, comfortable space where you won't be disturbed.

CLOSE your eyes and take some calming breaths. With your eyes closed, reflect on the Mercurial aspect of yourself—your fire, your goals. What makes you come alive? What do you know in your soul that you want? Open your eyes and write what Mercury looks like for you, in your life.

CLOSE your eyes again and reflect on the Sulfuric aspect of yourself—your contentment, your water. What brings you into the moment? How are you gentle with yourself? Open your eyes and write about what your Sulfur side looks like.

READ over what you've written. Can you see an imbalance between your Sulfur and Mercury sides? Was it easier to think about your goals or how you unwind? Are you more content or more striving? What step could you take to help balance these two sides of yourself? It could be as simple as taking more baths or writing to-do lists.

OVER the next few weeks, see if you can implement one step (only one!) to balance these two sides of yourself. Then repeat this exercise and see how your answers to the above questions compare.

Alchemy: Going Beyond the Elements

You now know the importance of the elements in alchemy, how they all spring (along with all other matter) from First Matter, and how they all come together to create the Philosopher's Stone in the Great Work. In chapter 3, we'll dive further into the Great Work, particularly looking into the three phases of alchemical transformation: the Blackening, or *Nigredo*; the Whitening, or *Albedo*; and the Reddening, or *Rubedo*. Prepare, budding alchemists, to go even deeper into the wacky world of alchemy.

CHAPTER 3

The Great Work
<u>of</u> Alchemy

Now, it may be easy to dismiss the Great Work of alchemy as being a bit antiquated. But, as you know by now, physical alchemy in a laboratory is just the beginning. If you want to change yourself, you must change your physical environment as well as do the inner work to change your leaden soul into a heart of gold.

We'll now dive into what this Great Work is all about and how it's still important to us modern alchemists.

Getting Into the Great Work

THE GREAT WORK ENCOMPASSES ALL FORMS OF ALCHEMICAL transformation: the purification of the spiritual self, mind, and physical world. In alchemy, the Great Work is the pursuit of the Philosopher's Stone. While the Philosopher's Stone is, according to alchemical lore, an actual stone (red and unpolished, if we're to believe Nicolas and Perenelle Flamel), it was also a means to purify all things. A universal solvent, the Philosopher's Stone can dissolve any substance into a liquid, acts as the elixir of life, can purify the body of aging, and turn lead into gold. In short, it is the apex of alchemy.

The Great Work is just that: work. It's the pursuit of perfection. As you've already learned, the Great Work is all about bringing together opposites: Sulfur and Mercury, male and female, the four elements, inner work and physical work. The Philosopher's Stone is the product of this union. In unifying all these opposing forces, the Philosopher's Stone is transformed back into First Matter, the basic building block of the world. Alchemists believed the Great Work begins and ends with First Matter. It's a belief symbolized in the Ouroboros: The serpent or dragon's head consumes its tail, symbolizing that with every end comes a new beginning.

It may sound counterintuitive for something to end where it begins, but this cyclical understanding of time and matter is present across cultures. According to the Hindu philosophy of *Brahman*, we all spring from First Matter (or *Brahman*) and all return to First Matter. Or, as the Old Testament reminds us, we "all are of the dust, and all turn to dust again."

Luckily for us, alchemists did their homework and were able to break down this tricky process. They identified three phases necessary for transformation: the Blackening, or *Nigredo*; the Whitening, or *Albedo*; and the Reddening, or *Rubedo*. The Seven Stages of alchemical transformation are divided among these three color-coded phases. Each phase, Black, White and Red, purifies matter, but does so in dramatically different ways.

Understanding the Three Phases of the Great Work

ET'S EXPLORE JUST HOW EACH PHASE CONTRIBUTES TO THE Great Work. In the Blackening, the substance is reduced to its most basic form by first being burned to ashes and then being further purified into a liquid solution. In the Whitening, the substance is separated from its baser parts, and then transformed into an altogether new form. In the Reddening, the substance is "resurrected" with fermenting bacteria and further purified beyond the Blackening and Whitening until reaching its highest form.

If you start looking, you'll see the Black, White, and Red phases play out in everyday transformations all around you, everything from cleaning lettuce to make a salad to quitting a job that you hate to find one that you love.

Let's look at that last example. Before you decide to quit your job, you need to have what Jung called the "dark night of the soul," during which you acknowledge that the job you're in is no longer working for you. This is the Blackening. Then you quit and have to figure out what you want to do next. This period is the Whitening. Then, you get some external "spark." Perhaps it's serendipitous, such as someone reaching out to you about an opportunity or coming across the perfect job listing online. Whatever form the spark takes, you look into it and eventually find the right path. This is the Reddening.

As with all things in alchemy, the colors (black, white, and red) and their order carry significance. Alchemists identified the color black with the "soot" or impurities of a substance. It's also traditionally a color associated with death and decomposition, a particularly potent association because decomposition converts impurities back into raw material. Black also comes about in physical alchemy, for when base metals are melted down together, they result in a black alloy.

White, on the other hand, is the opposite of black. In the Whitening, the "soot" from the Black Phase is discarded. In Christianity and some other

Torment of the Metals
S. Trismosin, Splendor solis, London, 16th century
Here, the King dismembers the body to separate the pure from the impure. He only takes the pure, golden head with him. The rest must be discarded.

religions, white is associated with purity, innocence, and even God, embodied in a white dove.

White also naturally occurs during specific alchemical laboratory experiments. If the black alloy from the first phase were to be heated with silver and then with mercury the resulting alloy would transform from black to white—hence, the Whitening.

It's during the Reddening, the final phase, that some divine spark breathes new life into the substance of study. In this phase, the substance finally succeeds in reaching its highest potential. Red is the color of life, of blood. Thomas Aquinas associated the color red with love. The association of red with love is indicative of how opposites come together in the Sacred Marriage. For many centuries, red, not black, was seen as the opposite of white. In this way, red is like a return to black, just as the Great Work begins and ends with First Matter. What is life but a big Ouroboros, after all? From dust we come, and to dust we return.

In the laboratory, when the white alloy from the second phase is combined with the two opposing forces of Sulfur and Mercury, the color changes to red, and that's how the Flamels legendarily ended up with a red Philosopher's Stone.

Alchemists are notorious secret keepers, making the three phases of the Great Work not always the easiest to untangle. Luckily for you, I'm neither Roger Bacon nor Jabir, and in the rest of the chapter we'll break down the Blackening, Whitening, and Reddening.

The Black Phase

The **Black Phase**, or *Nigredo,* is where the impurities of the spiritual self, mind, or matter are revealed. The Blackening is where we face our "shadow," the parts of ourselves we like to pretend aren't there. Alchemists considered the Blackening the most time-intensive phase of the Great Work. Alchemists compared it to being surrounded by an impenetrable black cloud. When the clouds are darkest, you don't know where you are or what you're doing. Then, when you feel utterly lost, the clouds clear, and you finally emerge into the Whitening transformed. When life feels bleakest, that's when true transformation occurs. In alchemy, despair, anxiety, and depression are endured in the Blackening with the knowledge that they'll lead you toward the White Phase.

Alchemists defined the Blackening as "mortification," which was associated with the "putting of things to death" in the Middle Ages. The Blackening is like a death of oneself, where matter, ego, identity, and the spiritual self all break down into their essential parts. Alchemists see the Blackening as the "torment of the metals" where burning, calcification, and decay allow a substance's superfluous parts to fall away. What's left behind is a thing's essence.

The alchemical symbol for Blackening is the black crow. According to Greek mythology, the god Apollo transformed his messenger crow from white to black in anger when the crow told him how his lover Koronis had taken another paramour. Apollo, enraged, sent his sister, Artemis, to kill Koronis. While Koronis's body was incinerated on the funeral pyre, Apollo took their son, the hero and god of medicine Asklepios, from her womb. For alchemists, the myth speaks to how the "impure" Koronis is burned away, leaving behind the pure child Asklepios. The same process occurs in the Blackening.

PHYSICAL ALCHEMY

The Blackening encompasses two stages of alchemical transformation: Calcination and Dissolution. In physical alchemy, the flame of Calcination reduces a substance to ashes. This flame is the hottest used in the Great Work, and alchemists compare it to the "dragon who drinks the water." In Calcination, the volatility of water is driven out of the substance so it becomes a solid or Salt. Some alchemists use a "liquid fire," such as acids or corrosive chemicals, in Calcination.

In Dissolution, the second stage of the Blackening, the ashes are dissolved in a liquid solvent. Maria Prophetissa's *tribikos* and Kleopatra's alembic, or

The Black Sun
S. Trismosin, Splendor solis, London, 16th century
The Black Sun in this late medieval depiction is a symbol for the alchemical stage of the Blackening. The dark sun must burn away impurities and purify what's left behind.

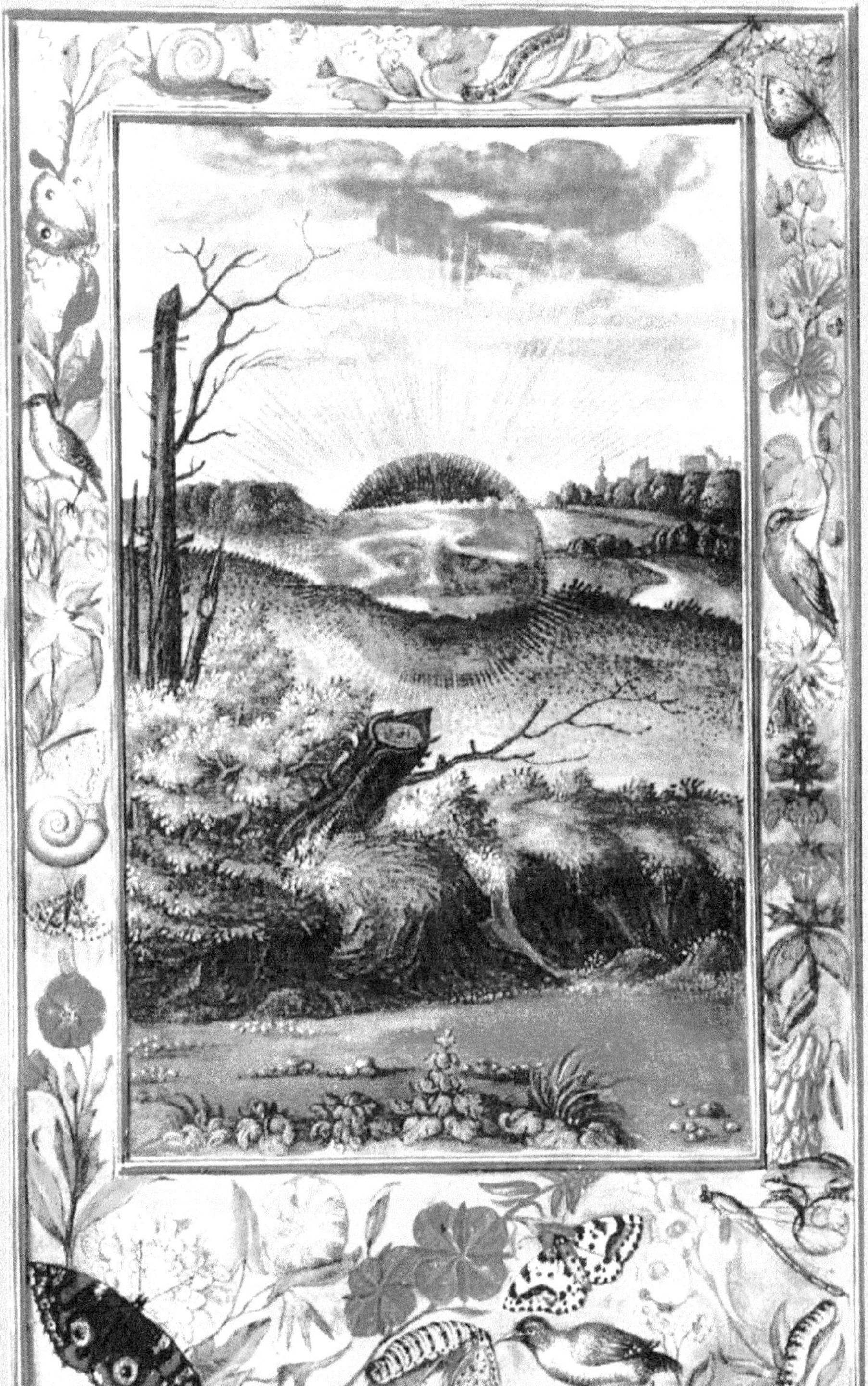

stillhead, both served important roles in the Dissolution process (as well as the Distillation).

SPIRITUAL ALCHEMY

In spiritual alchemy, Blackening was all about removing the impure parts of your soul and spirit. In the 16th century, John of the Cross wrote the mystical text *The Dark Night*, describing how the spiritual self must survive the darkness before being purified and unified with God. The Old Testament's Book of Job also speaks to the purification process necessary in the Blackening. Satan does everything in his power to turn Job from God; Job loses his servants, his fortune, even his children. Yet, Job holds on to the purity within himself, his faith in God, until God restores all that Job has lost and more.

Other ideas of Blackening exist in Eastern religions as well. The Buddha Siddhartha willingly gave up all his earthly possessions in search of enlightenment beneath the Bodhi tree. In Japanese mysticism, the Yamabushi live atop mountains, withdrawing from the world to find their purest selves. It can be scary to be alone. When we're completely alone for extended periods of time, without our phones or any distraction, we're forced to face aspects of ourselves we often try to hide. Hikers such as Cheryl Strayed talk about how the intensity of being alone on months-long hikes purifies oneself. This act of retreating into nature is like the fire of Calcination. Suddenly, there is nothing between you and your worst demons.

Spiritual Blackening is all about working through your darkest emotions. Emotions are traditionally thought to spring from the spiritual self, whereas thoughts spring from the mind and are therefore associated with mental alchemy. We all carry emotional baggage that weighs us down. In the Blackening, you have to sit with emotions as they come. Don't try to think your way around difficult emotions; instead, simply be with them. By acknowledging your negative emotions, you'll find that your emotional suitcase starts to feel a bit lighter. Just sitting with whatever negativity arises burns that negativity away to reveal your purer, truer self.

MENTAL ALCHEMY

In mental alchemy, Blackening is where you break down all the detrimental thought patterns that have snuck into your mind, usually without you even knowing. This is the time to interrogate all the assumptions you've adopted, whether from the media, education, external forces, or random things your family or friends have told you. We are all fed stories about everything, from how girls should wear their hair to who started a given war. Culture is like the rain; if you go outside, you're bound to get wet. Culture and history inundate us with all sorts of biases. The Blackening is where you work through those false beliefs so that your mind can become your own, free from all those outside influences.

Jung thought of the Blackening as the "dark night of the soul," when the ego and identity break down. It's when we meet our "shadow," our dark side. In mental Calcination, the mind becomes roasted in its own juices. We are forced to suffer through each of our demons, all of the biases we'd rather not have, the assumptions we've unfairly made, until none are left. Are you beginning to see why alchemists considered this the hardest phase of the transformation? Who wants to face all the nasty parts of themselves?

It's important to note here that going through the Blackening doesn't remove the darkness, but it rather reveals the dark light within. Blackening brings together the dark and the light of both the mind and the spiritual self. The goal is not to conquer your shadow, but to accept it as a part of yourself.

While mental Calcination deals with the conscious mind, mental Dissolution deals with the subconscious mind. This is where the work of understanding our dreams, daydreams, visions, or whatever else emerges from our subconscious mind comes into play. In the Blackening, you must remove the "soot" of both the conscious and unconscious minds.

If you're successful in physical, spiritual, and mental Blackening, then you're ready to embark on the next phase, the Whitening.

Alchemy Applied

A Personal Blackening:

A Meditation

MATERIALS
Glass of Water

IN this exercise, we'll use some mental alchemy to transform self-doubt into self-assuredness.

FILL a clear glass with purified, drinking water. Ideally choose a glass that means something to you, something you don't use everyday.

FIND a comfortable, quiet space where you won't be disturbed. Take an easy, seated posture where you can have a straight spine.

PLACE the glass of water in front of you.

TAKE a few calming breaths. Focus your attention on the glass of water. When your mind wanders gently bring your attention back to the water.

ONCE you feel your mind settle, pour all of your negative thoughts into the glass of water—your feelings of inadequacy, self-doubt, your anxieties. Imagine the water turning thick and black.

LIFT the glass, imagining all that negativity transforming into its true, purified state. Drink the whole glass, allowing the water to wash through you. Feel the water transform your negativity into self-assuredness, hope, and the knowledge that you are enough.

SMILE.

The White Phase

The **White Phase**, or *Albedo,* is where the pure is separated from the impure and then transformed into an altogether new compound. Removing impurities in the Blackening reveals the inherent duality of the mind, the spiritual self, and all matter. In alchemy, passive, watery Sulfur (the White Queen) and active, fiery Mercury (the Red King) embody this duality. In the second stage of the Whitening, known as Conjunction, these opposing forces are recombined. It's in the Whitening that the White Queen and Red King consummate their marriage and conceive the alchemical child.

The Whitening is about gently taking the tortured self or matter that has survived the Black Phase and cleansing it of the "shadow." Again, this doesn't mean removing the shadow. Instead, it means welcoming it into your purest, distilled self (such as accepting that you tend to run a few minutes behind any given schedule). If the Blackening is the darkest moments before the dawn, then the Whitening is when the first rays of the sun appear.

Alchemists related the Whitening to Aurora, the Roman goddess of the dawn, who emerges from the "black cloud" of the Blackening. The late-14th-century text *Aurora consurgens,* Latin for "the rising dawn," talks metaphorically about the end of the depressed state brought on by the Blackening and the beginning of the enlightenment that comes with the Whitening's metaphorical morning. In the 16th-century alchemical manuscript the *Splendor solis*, the Blackening, symbolized by the black sun, transforms into the rising sun of dawn in the Whitening.

PHYSICAL ALCHEMY

In physical alchemy, the Whitening encompasses two of the seven stages of alchemical transformation: Separation and Conjunction. Separation, or *separatio,* is when the liquid from Dissolution is filtered and the matter's pure essence is extracted.

The ancient Egyptians witnessed a natural Separation every year on the banks of the Nile. When lake beds dried up, Egyptian alchemists noticed a white salt residue was left behind. Egyptians called the white

54

compound *Natron*. This white residue is yet another reason that the second phase of alchemy is referred to as the Whitening. Alchemists would often use a screen or porous paper in Separation. Other Separation methods, such as skimming, sifting, or settling, could also be used.

The Conjunction, or *conjunctio,* is when the purified matter of Separation takes on a new form. Alchemists would mix the saved matter from Separation with a catalyst or acid. Only if the Conjunction produced an entirely new compound would the Whitening be deemed a success. The failure to produce a new compound meant that alchemists had to start over, as some flaw had remained behind after the Blackening.

If the Conjunction was successful, alchemists referred to the resulting compound as the **Child of the Conjunction**, or the **alchemical child**. The child is often considered a hermaphrodite, to symbolize the union of opposites in the Whitening. The child is the product of the union of the Red King and White Queen's Sacred Marriage, which I'll discuss in detail later in this chapter.

SPIRITUAL ALCHEMY

In spiritual alchemy, the Whitening represents the light that people report seeing during near-death experiences. It's the intermediary stage between life and the afterlife, where the soul and spirit are purified. Remember that the soul, or *animus,* is the constant, contented force within, symbolized by the White Queen. The spirit, or *spiritus,* is the striving, energetic force within, symbolized by the Red King.

If the Blackening is successful, the soul and spirit emerge cleansed. Emotional baggage no longer weighs you down because you've accepted your shadow in the Blackening. The light in your soul and spirit begins to shine now in the Whitening. You feel more content and can balance working toward goals with self-compassion and ease. You're not overly attached to particular outcomes. You can balance the interplay between the part of yourself striving toward betterment and the part of yourself that just wants to be here now.

Aurora

S. Trismosin, Splendor solis, London, 16th century

The red sun depicted in this 16th century alchemical manuscript denotes the rising purity in the material of study. The sun's red color is indicative of the final phase of transformation, the Red Phase. The black sun of the Blackening has now transformed into its purest form, the red rising sun of dawn.

In spiritual Blackening, you sit with and work through your negative emotions. In spiritual Separation, you must let go and discard the judgment of your shadow. In spiritual Conjunction, you combine your soul and spirit into a new spiritual self. This work is done in the heart, the emotional center of the body. If you're successful in combining your soul and spirit, you'll feel your heart open up. In Eastern traditions, the Whitening is akin to cleansing your heart chakra, opening yourself up to the realms of higher wisdom.

Christian alchemists understood spiritual Conjunction to be an alchemical crucifixion during which the spirit and soul are nailed (or take on a new form) between what is below (the world) and what is above (the divine). The crucifix represents the coming together of opposing forces in a new, purified form. The union of above and below goes all the way back to Thoth and the ancient alchemical text he supposedly wrote, the **Emerald Tablet**.

MENTAL ALCHEMY

In mental alchemy, the Whitening is all about further cleansing yourself of the assumptions and biases revealed in the Blackening. Through this continued purification in the Whitening, the mind takes on a new, higher form. During the Blackening, you've done the hard, necessary work of revealing your conscious and subconscious biases. You've faced your shadow self, and have seen the dark light within.

In mental Separation, you must sort through what parts of your personality and what assumptions are pure and which are not. What beliefs do you hold that are truly your own? Which of your habits are beneficial and make you feel good? What thought patterns can you let go of? When you berate yourself for burning dinner and think, "I'm such an idiot," does that reflect how you want to really relate to yourself? Consider these moments deeply and notice what sorts of thoughts you want to allow into your mind and which ones you want to let go of. Let go of judgment. This is the work of Whitening.

The work of combining all those opposing parts of yourself into a new mind or personality happens next in mental Conjunction. How do you make a new mind? By choosing the thoughts you allow to take up space. This is when your new identity takes shape—an identity not based on the assumptions you've adopted from society, but one that reflects who you truly are.

At the end of the Whitening, you'll probably find you have very few assumptions or biases left. You'll ask more questions and know fewer things to be true. You're only the fetus of the alchemical child, and so you should feel like a child, merely experiencing life, free of opinions or assumptions.

Now, this is hard work. More often than not the child of Conjunction struggles, and you'll discover that you still have more impurities (more biases, more negative emotions, more judgment) to work through before continuing to the Reddening. Or you'll find that your new mental attitude can't survive the everyday trials of difficult bosses or jury duty. Don't let this discourage you. Alchemical transformation is a process, and not an easy one. But just working toward your best, highest self is its own reward.

The Red Phase

The Red Phase, or *Rubedo,* is a continuation of the purification work done in the Whitening. Often, the Whitening and Reddening are seen as partners in the same process. The Red Phase continues what was started in the White Phase. This is embodied in the association of the White Queen to the Whitening and the Red King to the Reddening. In alchemical illustrations throughout history, the pair are often shown holding hands or holding alchemical equipment aloft. This serves to further emphasize the cooperation between the two phases they represent.

Sometimes alchemists add an intermediary stage, known as the **Yellowing**, between the Whitening and the Reddening. This short Yellowing stage, sometimes called *citrinas* or *xanthosis*, refers to a moment when the substance became yellow or golden in color. This brief change served as an indication that the alchemist was on the right track, that if they kept working they'd successfully turn a base metal into gold. Generally, alchemists consider the Red Phase to be inclusive of the Yellowing, so that's the approach I've taken here.

By the time the Red Phase rolls around, you'll likely feel pretty drained, having endured the torture of the Black Phase and the exhaustive purging of the White Phase. The Red Phase, therefore, begins with an external spark to the matter/self, like jumpstarting a metaphysical car. This is another moment when fire plays an important role. As in the Blackening, where the waters of Dissolution follow the fires of Calcination, water follows fire in the Reddening. After the spark of Fermentation, the substance is further purified in water until finally it arrives at the ultimate stage of the Reddening when, if everything goes according to plan, gold is produced and the Philosopher's Stone is achieved.

PHYSICAL ALCHEMY

The Red Phase encompasses the three final stages of alchemy: Fermentation, Distillation, and Coagulation.

Fermentation is when the "fetus" of the Conjunction begins to mature and quicken with new life. In the laboratory, Fermentation meant adding fermenting bacteria to the matter to spark new life within the substance. Fire would gently heat the substance, ensuring that the bacteria could work its magic.

After the Blackening and Whitening, the substance actually begins to decay during this first stage of the Reddening. This natural decay of the substance instigates Fermentation in a process called putrefaction. In this moment of decay, sometimes called the **Peacock's Tail**, a rainbow of brilliant colors, is produced. Alchemists saw this as the final death of any impurities.

While Fermentation utilizes fire, Distillation reintroduces water and air to the substance. In Distillation, the substance is repeatedly evaporated and condensed. It's a process once again aided by Kleopatra's alembic and Hypatia's hydroscope, and it serves to further purify the matter.

The final stage of alchemical transformation, Coagulation, is when the substance takes on its highest form. This is when the Philosopher's

Alchemy Around THE Globe

The Great Work is Never Done

Physical (or exoteric) alchemy has been married to spiritual and mental (esoteric) alchemy. It's a union that we have the earliest author of alchemical texts, Zosimos of Panopolis, to thank for. Zosimos dedicated his life to achieving the Great Work, both in the laboratory and in his own life.

As an alchemist and Gnostic mystic who lived at the end of the third and beginning of the fourth centuries CE, Zosimos wrote about the transformation of lead into gold as the Great Work, and he worked with his student, Theosebeia, to achieve it in the laboratory.

As a Gnostic, Zosimos also aligned physical alchemy with the mystical principals so integral in mental and spiritual alchemy. Gnostics, like alchemists, believed that the divine was innate in all things. Alchemy is all about revealing that inner divinity of all matter.

Just as Zosimos worked with Theosebeia in the laboratory, he worked equally to purify his own spiritual self and mind. He was the first alchemist to really define the Great Work in terms of the purification of the spiritual self and mind in addition to the physical, a union at the heart of alchemy. Zosimos believed, along with many of the alchemists that came after him, that an alchemist had to purify themselves before they could transform earthly materials into their true, divine forms.

Stone is achieved and when the purified essence extracted throughout the six other stages takes on a "body." The unreal becomes real.

SPIRITUAL ALCHEMY

The Reddening in spiritual alchemy involves the highest purification of the soul and spirit.

Spiritual Fermentation begins with a brief moment of putrefaction or decay, when the spiritual self is cleansed of any final emotional baggage. (Remember, alchemists believed emotions arise from the spiritual self, and thoughts from the mind. This distinction is important when thinking about spiritual versus mental alchemy.) Then, a new spark reenergizes the spiritual self in spiritual Fermentation. This spark could be anything from reading some Eastern philosophy to going to therapy. Whatever form it takes, this spark is always something external that enlivens your soul and spirit.

Fermentation is a process closely linked to the divine. Many cultures worship gods and goddesses associated with fermentation, such as the Greek god of wine, Bacchus, or the Baltic god Rugutis, who instigated the fermentation process. The most common fermentation process is the fermenting of sugars into alcohol. Ancients believed alcohol was the true essence of the grapes, grain, honey, or whatever was used to create the alcohol, which is where we get the term "spirits." Fermentation was thought to reveal the true essence or "spirit" of wheat, for instance, producing vodka.

In spiritual Distillation, water and air soothe the heat from Fermentation. Distillation also continues to gently purify the spiritual self. This is where you need that external spark. Maybe you really take to heart what your therapist told you or something clicks in the Eastern philosophy book you've been reading. Usually what you end up realizing in Distillation is how interconnected everything is.

Then, finally in spiritual Coagulation, the soul and spirit become corporeal. The immaterial becomes material. This can be manifested in an aura of pure white light or the Christian halo that denotes a saint.

MENTAL ALCHEMY

In mental alchemy, the Reddening culminates in the pure, enlightened mind.

The putrefaction at the beginning of Fermentation is a last death of any negative thoughts you're still carrying around. Any biases that survived the Blackening naturally decay and fall away during putrefaction. These final biases are the hardest to let go of and usually involve truly accepting, and even understanding, incomprehensible ideas, such as death.

Then the Fermentation of the mind begins in ernest. Images or visions of the divine may bubble up to the mind from the spiritual self. These divine visions are indicative of the union of the mind and spirit/soul that occurs in the Reddening. You must marry your thoughts with your emotions.

In mental Distillation, your personality and identity are washed away. Gently and repeatedly, you bathe your thinking mind in the waters of Distillation, allowing thoughts to fall away. Toward the end of Distillation, the mind becomes quiet and completely present. When you contemplate the future, it doesn't bring you anxiety. When you contemplate the past, you don't have regrets. Instead, you are content and in the moment.

In Coagulation, the purified mind merges with the spiritual self and is made corporeal. This material form becomes a halo or aura of light known as the **Ultimate Material**, or *ultima materia*. The Ultimate Material is the mental and spiritual Philosopher's Stone. It's fixed. No external events can steal this divine light once it is achieved. In the same way that neither Christian saints nor Buddhist bodhisattvas can lose their holiness or enlightenment, neither can you if the Coagulation of your mind and spiritual self are successful.

The Sacred Marriage

The turning point of any alchemical transformation is when opposing forces are unified in the Sacred Marriage, which occurs at the end of the Whitening and beginning of the Reddening during Conjunction. The union of opposing forces gives rise to an altogether new compound known as the child of the Conjunction or the alchemical child. During

The Sacred Marriage or *Conjunctio*
S. Trismosin, Splendor solis, London, 16th century
The White Queen and the Red King are about to take hands, symbolizing the Sacred Marriage. The White Queen stands upon the moon, while the Red King stands upon the flames of the sun. The royals' relationship to the moon/night and sun/day demonstrates that this is a marriage of opposites, a union of opposing forces.

the Conjunction, the child is a fetus and needs to further mature before it can survive being born into the world at the end of the Reddening.

Symbolically, the **Sacred Marriage** is the union between the White Queen and the Red King. The **White Queen** is the soul, or *animus,* and it is associated with the Whitening. She is content and symbolized by the moon and water. She is Sulfur. The **Red King** is the spirit, or *spiritus*. He is energetic and striving toward goals and self-improvement. He's associated with the sun, the element of fire, and the Reddening. He is Mercury, the alchemical opposite of Sulfur.

Opposites have always fascinated alchemists. While much of recorded history has negated feminine energy, alchemists have always acknowledged the importance of the White Queen. After all, the Great Work is possible only when the feminine energy of the White Queen is balanced with the masculine energy of the Red King to produce the alchemical child.

As I've previously mentioned, the alchemical child is a hermaphrodite. Oftentimes the child is depicted with two heads, a man's and a woman's, as well as both sexes' genitalia. Another name for the child is **rebis**, which comes from the Latin *res bina,* or "double-thing." The word "hermaphrodite" itself actually comes from the female "Aphrodite," the Greek goddess of love, and the male "Hermes," the Greek messenger of the gods, known as Mercury to the Romans.

"Isn't Mercury associated with the masculine?" you may ask, or "Didn't you say that the White Queen is Sulfur?" I did. Now, remember way back in chapter 2, when I said that sometimes alchemists contradicted themselves and would associate spirit with the feminine and soul with the masculine? The same is true here. These two opposing forces are unnamable, so calling one feminine and one masculine is ultimately limiting and inaccurate.

PHYSICAL ALCHEMY

One of the most interesting little-known facts about alchemy is that often alchemists worked with a partner of the opposite gender. Nicolas Flamel worked with his wife, Perenelle. The Arabian alchemist Zosimos worked with his student (and possibly his sister), Theosebeia. The 17th-century alchemist Thomas Vaughan worked with his wife, Rebecca. Christina of Sweden worked with several male alchemists, including Giuseppo Francesco Borri. These partnerships were a way for alchemists to personify the Sacred Marriage in the laboratory before even picking up an alembic.

Chemically speaking, the Sacred Marriage in physical alchemy is embodied in the new compound created in Conjunction. Conjunction was seen as the union of the elements fire, water, and air to create a new "earth" compound. Beyond just the Great Work, there is a host of different alchemical experiments that support the notion that an altogether new substance can be created from the union of opposites. Remember, alchemists did a lot of things in their laboratories other than just trying to accomplish the Great Work and make the Philosopher's Stone. They had all sorts of wild experiments!

For instance, in an eighth-century experiment, alchemists combined salt and sulfuric acid to create nitrohydrochloric acid, a liquid capable of dissolving gold and platinum. Jabir developed the experiment, calling the resulting yellow-orange liquid "royal water." Now, in the age of modern chemistry, it's common knowledge that combining two substances can create a new compound. But in the Middle Ages, such alchemical experiments could garner accusations of witchcraft and even get you burned at the stake, no matter how incredible your discovery.

SPIRITUAL ALCHEMY

In spiritual alchemy, the Sacred Marriage is the union of the soul and spirit. Alchemists thought of it as an inner marriage, even calling it an incestuous marriage between our two selves—a statement the Catholic Church wasn't too keen on, as you might imagine. (The Church had its reasons for decrying alchemy as heretical in the Middle Ages, though. Alchemy was like its own religion in many ways.) Nonetheless, the idea in spiritual alchemy is that this is a marriage of your striving, energetic spirit and your more content, present soul.

This is no easy task, as you might imagine. No one can constantly be striving toward their goals and be present simultaneously. You'd drive yourself crazy. So, how do you reconcile the two? How do you marry the striving spirit and the present soul?

In alchemy, it all comes down to balance. We must balance these two necessary parts of ourselves. Whenever you're feeling stressed or anxious, it's likely an indication that your soul and spirit are unbalanced. When your spirit and soul are married, you can work toward goals without chasing them.

Our minds and brains love to think far into the future, which is usually where the anxiety and stress stems from. But, when it comes to goals, there are small steps you can take to move toward that future. Don't stress about needing to buy a house. Instead, think about a small step you can take to be ready to buy a house, such as getting your finances in order. You might find that accomplishing the smaller goal feels just as good as the big lofty goal. By focusing on smaller goals that are easier to accomplish, you'll find that you're more present and less stressed. Smaller goals mean you're working with your striving spirit and also giving yourself more space to be content and present with your soul.

MENTAL ALCHEMY

The Sacred Marriage in mental alchemy is seen as the perfect union of the conscious and unconscious minds. According to Jung, this union gives rise to wholeness that he called the archetypal Self. Jung's last book before his death, *Mystery of the Conjunction*, was all about the Sacred Marriage. Jung equated the unconscious mind with the White Queen and the conscious mind with the Red King.

Bringing together the conscious and unconscious minds in the Sacred Marriage, Jung believed, could prompt visions and vivid dreams. Jung described his own visions of the Sacred Marriage as ecstatic, beautiful, and unencumbered by time. Jung's visions allowed his identity to fall away and for him to be fully present.

Modern psychologists consider the Sacred Marriage a "peak experience" in which the oneness of the universe becomes clear and you let go of your identity, an idea first put forward by the psychologist Abraham Maslow. Maslow's peak experiences are quite similar to Jung's mental Sacred Marriage, as both are out of time, out of body, deeply fulfilling, and euphoric. In mental alchemy, the union of your conscious and unconscious minds brings about the happiness and fulfillment of a peak experience.

But how do you unify your conscious mind and your unconscious mind? Like in the Blackening, this is the work of removing the "soot," the unnecessary assumptions and beliefs that usually come from society and the world around us. This work brings what was previously unconscious to the conscious mind, melding the two. There's also a need for acceptance that there are some aspects of yourself, of your unconscious mind, that aren't going to change. You're never going to fully be able to comprehend death or remember your birth. You have to hold space for what's unknowable.

Alchemy:
Both Great AND Granular

Now that you have a firm grasp on the three phases of the Great Work, you're well on your way! Looking back through these pages, we've covered *a lot* of ground. In chapter 1, we covered the more than 2,000-year-old history of alchemy and looked at the three main facets of alchemy (physical, spiritual, and mental). Then, in chapter 2, we got into all things elemental, from where elements came from and what they represent to their roots in First Matter and union in the Philosopher's Stone. Here in chapter 3, we did a deep dive into the Great Work, its three phases, and the importance of the Sacred Marriage.

With all of Part I serving as our foundation, we're now ready to hop into Alchemy 201. In Part II, we'll explore how alchemy ties into everything grand (such as the planets and cosmos) and granular (how alchemy influences everything from modern science, art, and literature), showing how even now alchemy influences our day-to-day lives.

PART II

ALCHEMY IN ALL THINGS GREAT AND SMALL

It's time to dive into how alchemy is applicable to everything great and small. We'll be exploring how alchemists worked with the planets and universe, meticulously timing experiments to the movement of the cosmos. Then we'll examine all the ways alchemy and its principles continue to influence the disciplines of chemistry, psychology, art, and literature today. We can see alchemy all around us if we take a moment to look for it.

CHAPTER 4

Alchemy and
THE Planets

Humans have always looked up at the night sky and contemplated their place in the cosmos. Ancient Sumerian clay tablets recorded daily observations of the moon and planets. Ancient Babylonians made observations of phenomenon we're still looking up at in wonder, like Halley's Comet and eclipses.

Alchemy and astrology have been linked ever since the two disciplines emerged back in the ancient world. In alchemy, almost every aspect of physical and metaphysical existence aligns with the seven ruling planets. Elements, metals, days of the week, and parts of the human body all correspond to specific planets. Likewise, alchemists believed the Seven Stages of alchemical transformation corresponded with the seven planets of ancient and medieval astronomy.

Climbing ㉞ Ladder
㉝ the Planets

CLIMBING THE LADDER OF THE PLANETS WAS ANOTHER WAY TO conceptualize the Great Work. Climbing the Ladder meant ascending toward physical and metaphysical perfection, as each of the seven ruling planets (Saturn, Jupiter, Mars, Venus, Mercury, Moon, and Sun) correspond with one of the Seven Stages of alchemy. When pursuing the Great Work, alchemists would pass through each planet's "rung," and so the **Ladder of the Planets** was born.

This association between the planets and the Seven Stages was embodied in the ancient teachings of Thoth: "As above, so below." Alchemists believed their laboratories were microcosms of the universe. By practicing alchemy, alchemists were in league with God and worked to mirror God's perfection in the laboratory.

In addition to believing each planet corresponded with one of the Seven Stages of transformation, alchemists also believed each planet corresponded with one of the seven metals of alchemy (lead, tin, iron, copper, quicksilver, silver, and gold). Thus, climbing the Ladder of the Planets also reflected the progression of lead (Saturn) into gold (Sun).

The association between the cosmos above and the individual below went beyond just physical alchemy. Ancient astronomers and alchemists saw the human body as a self-contained, shrunken reflection of the cosmos. They believed we are all made of the same stuff as the universe, which scientists and astronomers have actually proven to be true. All of us (along with our cats, dogs, and all the other organisms of the Earth)

Ladder of the Planets
S. Michelspacher,
Cabala, Augsburg, 1616
Here, the blindfolded, ignorant alchemist must find the seven steps of alchemical transformation. The dome depicted in the center of this image symbolizes the union of opposites that ultimately results in the phoenix, a symbol of the utmost purity, perched atop the dome. On the hill surrounding the dome, various gods, each associated with a planet, stand watch. Encircling the whole image is the zodiac and four elements, which are vital to a successful transformation.

contain carbon, nitrogen, and oxygen atoms in our bodies that came from stars that exploded 4.5 billion years ago.

Climbing the Ladder of the Planets in mental and spiritual alchemy meant climbing from the baseness of Saturn to the perfection of the Sun. In Alexandria during the second century CE, the early Christian scholar, ascetic, and theologian Origenes first conceptualized the Ladder of the Planets. His writings speak to a celestial ladder with seven gates, and how the psyche would pass through each gate on their way to divine perfection.

This parallel between the individual and the cosmos is the basic principle of astrology. When you read your horoscope, you're buying into the alchemical idea that the planets and their movements affect us. Just as alchemy cannot be disentangled from astronomy, ancient astronomy is twisted up in astrology, too. It wasn't until the 17th century that the "hard," rigorous sciences of chemistry and astronomy were separated from their mystical forebearers, alchemy and astrology.

Still, it's important to draw the distinction that the Ladder of the Planets is a uniquely alchemical concept. Astrology, like other ancient metaphysical pursuits, looks at how the heavens above affect us earthlings below. "Mercury is going into retrograde, o esteemed king. It's probably a bad time to invade France," the astrologers of the English court might have warned. Alchemists, however, saw the planets charting a path toward perfection. Alchemists were interested not in daily horoscopes but in achieving lifelong perfection. "Drink this tonic on the full moon, o king, and send prayers to God asking to heal your sickness," the English alchemists might advise their king. A bit different from counseling against the invasion of France, no?

Now, you've probably already wised up to the fact that the Ladder of the Planets doesn't have the same number of planets we think of today. Indeed, the Ladder of the Planets is missing a few important ones—sorry, Uranus and Neptune—and includes nonplanets, the Sun and Moon. The reason alchemists and ancient astronomers settled on these seven planets is simply because they were the ones they could see. Uranus wasn't discovered until 1781, and it took more than 80 years after that to notice poor Neptune floating around in the night sky. The Sun and Moon were likewise included in the Ladder because they could be seen.

Ancient alchemists and astronomers observed how the Moon passed each planet in turn. It was as if the Moon were climbing a ladder of planets every 28 days, and so alchemists developed the concept. It's also thought that the order of the planets in the Ladder may be based on brightness, starting with the darkest planet, Saturn, to the brightest, the Sun. This brightness theory also corresponds with the alchemical transformation from the darkness of the Blackening to the inner light and "brightest" gold in the Reddening.

In the rest of this chapter, we'll take a look at each planet of the Ladder, its associations, and how it relates to the alchemical process.

Saturn

In alchemy, Saturn is the lowest rung in the Ladder of the Planets, but don't let that make you think any less of Saturn. As the starting point of transformation, Saturn holds the same duality that First Matter does. It is both raw matter and the energy necessary for transformation. It represents the most noble and regal of all the planets and is associated with the base metal lead.

Alchemists considered Saturn to be a "black Sun." It was a reflection of the Sun at the top of the Ladder. The Ladder begins and ends with the Sun. The connection between Saturn and the Sun is akin to how transformation begins and ends with First Matter, a concept symbolized in the Ouroboros.

Saturn is associated with the color black and Calcination, the first stage of the Black Phase.

Alchemists also believed that different planets were associated with different parts of the body, a belief that stemmed from the notion that our bodies reflect the cosmos. Saturn was associated with the spleen, teeth, and bones, parts of the body that are seen as the core of existence. The spleen was thought to house ill-tempered, "base" emotions, such as spite and anger. Teeth and bones likewise provide the skeleton that the rest of the body is built upon.

Astrologically speaking, Saturn is associated with Capricorn and Aquarius. Capricorns are grounded, reliable, and practical. Earth-sign Capricorns excel at keeping their worlds in order. Those of the air sign Aquarius, on the other hand, are independent, intelligent, friendly, and love to travel. They seek out transformative experiences through outlets such as religion, therapy, and meditation. Considering the duality in First Matter, Capricorn resembles the real, tangible, raw matter of the universe, whereas Aquarius mirrors the transformative energy of First Matter. In other words, Saturn, as in all things in alchemy, is a product of opposites.

In mythology, Saturn maintains this duality as well, being portrayed either as the winged god of time or a sinister old king about to fall from his throne. In Greek mythology, Saturn is Cronus, the father who must fall in order for Zeus to rise. And Zeus just so happens to be associated with the next Ladder rung, Jupiter.

Jupiter

Jupiter is the second rung of the Ladder, associated with the metal tin and the alchemical stage Dissolution. While Saturn violently burns away the pure from the impure in Calcination, Jupiter is the levelheaded judge that finishes the job. Jupiter is the water of Dissolution that gently soothes and cleanses, and is the spirit that energizes the tortured soul that's survived the unforgiving Calcination of Saturn.

The ancients considered Jupiter the most favorable planet. Ancient Babylonians believed Jupiter occupied a revered place in the heavens because the planet drifts in and out of view in the night sky. Ancient Greeks thought Jupiter instilled order in the universe, because it seemed to "wander" in the sky according to its own rules, unlike the other stars which seemed fixed.

In astrology, the planet Jupiter rules Sagittarius, the centaur poised with bow and arrow, who is the wise leader. While certainly conventionally intelligent, Sagittarian intelligence extends beyond the practical knowledge of Saturn and into the deep spiritual awareness of Jupiter.

The sensitive water sign Pisces is also ruled by Jupiter. As the planet of Dissolution, Jupiter holds space for empathy and compassion as the waters wash away any impurities not yet burned away in Calcination.

The myths around Saturn and Jupiter prove that Jupiter is, in the end, the better, "purer" ruler. In Greek mythology, Jupiter is Zeus, king of the Gods. Saturn (Cronus to the Greeks) is the prior king, so scared one of his children would usurp him that he devours them. Jupiter, who was saved by his mother, eventually forces his father to regurgitate all his brothers and sisters. Alchemists related this myth to how Dissolution purifies the ashes of Calcination, just as Jupiter purifies his father of his siblings.

Jupiter is also associated with the liver, an organ that purifies the body, filtering out toxins just like in Dissolution.

Mars

Mars is the third rung of the Ladder of the Planets. The metal associated with Mars is iron, fitting when you consider that iron deposits are actually what give Mars its red color (which, spookily, the alchemists would have had no way of knowing). The planet is literally covered in iron oxide, otherwise known as rust. Mars is also associated with war and violence, and iron was often the metal used for making swords and armor.

Mars is linked to the alchemical stage of Separation. Separation is where the pure is extracted from the impure. Mars (being a bit rowdy with all his warring) is the energetic impulse that initiates this separation.

Mars is equated with the Red King. In alchemy, Mars (the Red King) and Venus (the White Queen) consummate their relationship to produce the alchemical child or the child of Conjunction.

As we've already gleaned, the White and Red phases are closely linked, and their association is made especially clear when you take into consideration the alchemists' Ladder. According to the Ladder, there are not one but two moments when the Red King and White Queen consummate their relationship. The first is in the White Phase between the planets Mars and Venus. The second is in the Red Phase between the Sun and the Moon (more on that later.)

Mars takes on all of the traditional associations of the Red King: energetic, powerful, and striving. Mars is the spirit, and it is associated with material possessions, especially those necessary for survival.

In astrology, the planet Mars rules Aries. The fire sign Aries is active, competitive, decisive, and singular. Aries is the first sign of the zodiac, thought to be the energy that instigates spring when the Sun enters Aries in March (the month of Mars). To a lesser degree, Mars is also associated with the emotional drive and productivity of Scorpio. Even though Mars is primarily associated with the Red King, it has some of the contentment of the White Queen.

In Roman mythology, Mars is the god of war and consort of Venus. Mars has something like the god equivalent of ADHD and can never sit still. He's always raring for the next battle. In Greek and Roman myths, Venus always needed to calm him down to keep the peace between him and the other Olympians.

Mars is associated with the gallbladder, which was believed by the ancients to be associated with bravery and bold behavior. It's where we get the word "gall"—meaning rash, courageous behavior. Sounds just like Mars, doesn't it?

Venus

Venus is the fourth rung on the Ladder of the Planets. Venus's metallic association is copper, a highly malleable metal that's been around since 9000 BCE; it is perfect for shaping into jewelry and tools. Alchemists consider copper the "Harlot of the Metals" because it so easily combines with other metals. Brass, a metal commonly associated with Venus, is a mixture of copper and zinc. Bronze, another mixture of copper with tin, revolutionized humanity during the Bronze Age, because it was more durable than any other previously known metal. Venus's association with love and sexuality means the making of new metals sits comfortably in her wheelhouse.

Alchemists linked Venus with Conjunction, one of the most important stages in alchemy, which marks the consummation of the Red King and White Queen. The byproduct of their union is the fetus of the child of the Conjunction.

CONIVNCTIO SIVE
Coitus.

Unification or Copulation during the Sacred Marriage
Rosarium philosophorum, 1550
Here, the Red King and White Queen are shown consummating the Sacred Marriage. Notice the moon and sun in the waters, which symbolize that this marriage is a union of planetary opposites.

Venus likewise adopts many of the characteristics associated with the White Queen: receptive, magnetic, a gentle presence. While Venus represents one aspect of the union, the White Queen, she is also the union itself. This is because Venus appears both in the daylight of the morning and in the darkness of the night. Venus is, like the rebis, a double thing, considered energetic and striving during the day and receptive and content at night. She is both male and female, in this sense, just as Mars has a small aspect that is associated with the White Queen, due to the planet's association with the water sign Scorpio.

In astrology, Venus rules both Taurus and Libra. Earth-sign Taureans are driven and seek out what they want. They are sexual, patient, loyal, and reliable. Libras seek companionship and are fair judges, romantic, and hard workers. They tend to be dependable, cooperative and gracious, and they seek out beauty. Both Libras and Taureans seek out partnerships and move toward harmony and balance, just like Venus.

In mythology, Venus (known as Aphrodite to the Greeks) is the goddess of love and beauty. As the wife of the gods' blacksmith, Vulcan, and consort of Mars, Venus occupied a place of prominence in alchemy. She tempers Mars's rash behavior, which is why Venus is associated with the kidneys in addition to the sex organs. The ancients believed the kidneys controlled one's disposition, calming the erratic behavior housed in the gallbladder, which was associated with Mars. Venus is the receptive contentment of the White Queen and the kidneys as well as the alchemical child and sex organs.

The term "hermaphrodite" actually comes from another Greek myth, in which Aphrodite has a child named Hermaphroditus with Hermes. And Hermes (aka Mercury) just so happens to be the next planet on the Ladder. So Venus is the consort of both Hermes above her and Mars below her, making her one sexually liberated goddess!

Mercury

The fifth rung on the Ladder of the Planets is Mercury. Closest to the sun and the fastest planet in our solar system, Mercury's metal was known as quicksilver to alchemists, and today simply as mercury. The metal mercury actually got its name from the planet.

Quicksilver is a liquid at room temperature and is most often seen in its silvery, liquid form. Mercury has a rather erratic orbit in the sky, appearing to swing back and forth around the Sun. Alchemists associated the planet's irregular orbit with quicksilver's tendency to spill and difficulty to control in experiments. And so, quicksilver came to be known as mercury.

Mercury, like Venus, represents the duality of the alchemical child. Observed right before or after sunrise or sunset, the planet is visible only when the sky transforms from night to day or vice versa. Sunrise and sunset are both a mixture of night and day, moments when the sky expresses the inherent duality of matter.

The metal quicksilver likewise expresses the duality of the rebis. While alchemists believed the metal could grant everlasting life, it could also prove lethal. Quicksilver exists between the duality of life and death, as ancient Chinese alchemists had to figure out the hard way.

When the first emperor of China, Qin Shi Huang Di, fell gravely ill, ancient Qin dynasty alchemists thought they knew just what to do, and gave the emperor a mercury tonic they believed to be the elixir of life. Things didn't exactly pan out as planned, and the mercury-and-jade mixture ended up killing the emperor.

This duality between life and death also links the planet with the alchemical stage of Fermentation, where a gentle fire either pushes the child of Conjunction to mature or to become stillborn.

In astrology, Mercury rules Gemini and Virgo. Gemini, the twins, represents the duality of the self. Virgo, meanwhile, is the pure self that survives the fires of Fermentation.

In mythology, Mercury is the messenger god of travel, communication, and intellectual pursuits. The Greeks called him Hermes, and the Egyptians called him Thoth. Mercury is the patron of alchemy. He leads souls to the underworld, back to their original form as First Matter.

Mercury was associated with the lungs that breathe new life into alchemical transformation during Fermentation. The lungs were associated with the all-important bellows that kept the fires going in alchemical laboratories.

Mercury is also associated with the next planet in the Ladder, the Moon, because both have similar crater-marked surfaces.

The Moon

The Moon is the sixth rung of the Ladder. Like Venus, the Moon is associated with the White Queen. But where the union of Venus and Mars is a bodily, sexual union, the union between the Moon and Sun is a higher union of spirit and soul. The White Queen, or Luna, is usually shown standing on the Moon. The Moon is considered the sister to her brother, the Sun. Their union, therefore, is an incestuous one, symbolizing the unification of opposing forces within ourselves. But fear not, alchemists supported only *symbolic* incest.

The Moon is thought to rule the subconscious and the contented soul. Many cultures follow the 13-month lunar calendar when planting and harvesting crops, and they associate the Moon with fertility and the nurturing of the Earth and self.

The Moon is associated with silver, a metal that's been used in coins and jewelry since at least the fourth millennium BCE. Alchemists have long associated silver with the Moon because the planet and metal share a similar luster. The reflective nature of the metal was also associated with the Moon's influence over the tides. The Moon seems to work in harmony with nature, striking a balance that alchemists sought to replicate in their work.

Alchemists associate the Moon with the alchemical stage of Distillation, where air and water purify the matter and self. It's a gentle process in which the matter is coaxed toward its ultimate form in Coagulation. The Moon's association with fertility is akin to how alchemists gently nurture the matter and self toward their highest forms.

The Moon holds sway over all the zodiac signs, moving through all 12 signs every 28 days or so. The Moon's placement in the sky at the time of your birth determines your emotional life, such as what sort of romantic partner will suit you best.

In mythology, the Moon has taken on many guises. For the ancient Sumerians, Sin, the god of magic and the mystical arts, ruled the Moon. For the Greeks, the Titan Selene, the virgin goddess of the hunt Artemis, and the goddess of witchcraft Hecate all ruled the Moon. The many goddesses of the Moon in Greek mythology reflect the Moon's importance and inability to be tied into one form. The Moon is like water, shifting in and out of definition. This again highlights the difference between the Moon and Venus. Whereas Venus is associated with only one goddess, the Moon has many faces (both literally speaking and goddess speaking). The Moon is mutable, like the soul, while Venus is more bound to her single form.

In addition to being associated with the uterus, the Moon was also associated with the brain, the seat of human intellect that was closely linked with the heart and its planet, the Sun.

The Sun

The Moon's partner is the Sun, the highest rung on the Ladder of the Planets. The Sun is the brightest of all the celestial bodies, and is therefore associated with matter's highest form. Just as the Moon is a truer White Queen than Venus, the Sun is the truer Red King than its counterpart Mars. Mars and Venus's union is a sexual one, while the Moon and Sun's union is a spiritual partnership that produces the Philosopher's Stone, another alchemical concept associated with the Sun. In the same way that Venus is both the White Queen and the alchemical child, the Sun is the Moon's partner, the Red King, and the fruits of the Sun and Moon's union, the Philosopher's Stone.

When looking up at the sky from Earth, the Sun and Moon seem to be the same size. That's why the Moon can eclipse the Sun. Their similar size is one more way the Sun and Moon were linked for alchemists. In fact, alchemists considered a total solar eclipse to symbolize the Sacred Marriage between the Sun and Moon.

The Sun is associated with the highest metal, gold. Gold's been a precious metal since the end of the fifth millennium BCE, when ancient Egyptians first started using it in ornate jewelry. It's a highly malleable metal that doesn't tarnish. Its chemical symbol, Au, comes from the word *Aurora,* meaning "shining dawn," referring to gold's brilliant or "shining" appearance.

Alchemists associated the Sun with Coagulation, where the physical becomes metaphysical and vice versa. Coagulation marks the return to First Matter, where the dragon's tail enters its mouth in the Ouroboros.

Like the Moon, the Sun and its placement in the sky at your birth determine the expression of the 12 zodiac signs in your life. The Sun moves through all 12 signs over the course of a year. The Sun's position at your birth represents your individuality and personality, who you really are without all the biases we adopt from society.

In mythology, the Sun is both brother and lover to the Moon, again emphasizing that the alchemical Sacred Marriage is an incestuous one, marrying the opposites within oneself. In Egypt, the sun is associated with Osiris, husband to the lunar goddess Isis. In Greece, the Sun, like the Moon, has many associations. The Sun is the titan Helios, brother of Selene, the Moon. Apollo, Artemis's brother (and husband, according to pre-Hellenistic texts), is also associated with the Sun. But neither Artemis nor Apollo ever marry, because their union is a spiritual one, not a bodily one.

The Sun is associated with the heart, the chief and purest of the organs. It was thought to generate the heat needed for life, which only the brain (associated with the Moon) could cool.

The Alchemical Cosmos Chart Explored

AS YOU'VE LEARNED, THERE ARE MANY WAYS ALCHEMISTS work with the grandeur of the cosmos. To keep everything straight, you'll find a chart that organizes all the various planetary correspondences.

In the chart, you'll find the planet, its alchemical stage and concept, metal and zodiac associations, physical embodiment, color, elemental alignment, and day of the week. I've covered many of these associations above, but here you'll find new ones to explore.

Alchemists believed that different metals could purify different inner workings of the body. Remember how alchemists believed we all contained the cosmos within? Well, that's precisely how they came to associate different planets with various organs.

Planetary colors can come from specific colors that may arise during an alchemical stage, or just general associations with the planet. For instance, the Sun's color is purple because purple was considered the most royal and expensive of dyes. The same is true of elements associated with the planets. The Moon is associated with the element water because the Moon is the ruler of the tides.

The planets and their names also influence the days of the week, since we inherited our calendar mainly from the Romans.

Alchemists could use these various associations to amplify their work. For instance, they could choose to begin Calcination on Saturday. Or, they might have initiated Conjunction when Taurus was prominent in the sky. If you want to journal on your shadow and root out the "soot" like in the Blackening, maybe wear black when you do so, associating yourself with Saturn and the alchemical stage of Calcination. Get creative! There are no wrong answers here.

THE Alchemical Cosmos Chart

PLANET	ALCHEMICAL STAGE	ALCHEMICAL CONCEPT	METAL	ZODIAC SIGN
♄ SATURN	1 CALCINATION	First Matter, p. 32	Lead	♑ ♒ Capricorn, Aquarius
♃ JUPITER	2 DISSOLUTION	—	Tin	♐ ♓ Sagittarius, Pisces
♂ MARS	3 SEPARATION	The Red King, p. 63	Iron	♈ ♏ Aries, Scorpio
♀ VENUS	4 CONJUNCTION	The White Queen, p. 63 rebis	Copper/ Brass	♉ ♎ Taurus, Libra
☿ MERCURY	5 FERMENTATION	The Alchemical Child as "fetus", p. 63	Quicksilver	♊ ♍ Gemini, Virgo
☽ MOON	6 DISTILLATION	The White Queen, p. 63	Silver	♋ All, especially Cancer
☉ SUN	7 COAGULATION	The Red King, p. 63 Philosopher's Stone, p. 35	Gold	♌ All, especially Leo

DAY	ORGAN	COLOR	EMBODIMENT	ELEMENT
SATURDAY	Spleen, Teeth, Bones	● BLACK	Dark, benevolent	—
THURSDAY	Liver	○ YELLOW	Generous, justice	△ AIR
TUESDAY	Gallbladder	● RED	Active, masculine	🔥 FIRE
FRIDAY	Kidneys, sex organs	○ WHITE	Feminine, fertility, love	▽ EARTH
WEDNESDAY	Lungs	● BLUE	Eloquence, androgyny, mind	△ AIR
MONDAY	Brain, uterus	● GREEN	Night, purification, soul	≈ WATER
SUNDAY	Heart	● PURPLE	True self, energy, spirit	🔥 FIRE

Alchemy Applied

Your Shadow Self:

A Journal Exercise

MATERIALS

Pen or Pencil • Journal

REFLECT on your "shadow" self throughout the day. What moments were difficult or trying today? In the past week? In the last year? This should be a moment where you're not entirely proud of your actions or how you've reacted.

FIND a quiet, safe place where you can reflect and write, ideally in the evening, so you can reflect as the day comes to a close.

WRITE about one difficult or trying moment, or a recurring difficulty, that stands out in your memory. Think about the circumstances that contributed to that moment. How did you feel? What were you afraid of in that moment? Did you feel judged? Was that real or perceived? How does this moment fit into your past? Was there something triggering about this moment? Try to write quickly, without judgment. Just capture your thoughts stream of consciousness style. Set a timer for 10 minutes.

TAKE A BIG BREATH once the time is up. Put your hands over your heart, and imagine your hands burning away all your negativity around that experience. Imagine your hands purifying your body, soul, and mind of that experience.

WRITE a letter to yourself that would've made you feel better in that moment. Acknowledge that your past feelings around this event are totally and completely valid. Give yourself permission to act differently next time, to acknowledge the feelings, but know that you no longer have to act on them.

REREAD your letter whenever you feel those emotions or that experience bubble up in the future. Know your emotions are valid, and then breathe and let them go. Be kind to yourself; this is hard work!

Approaching THE Axis

In this chapter, we've gone both great and small, from learning about the Ladder of the Planets and how they align with classical mythology to how there's more to the alchemical cosmos than meets the eye! You've even had the chance to journal deeply into your shadow self, exploring how you act and react to things through the alchemical lens.

Now, we'll have the chance to glimpse not only how far alchemy extends back into history, but how its influences stretch beyond its assumed boundaries. From literature to art to matters of the mind, as you'll soon see, alchemy touches far more that might surprise you.

CHAPTER 5

The Axis OF Alchemy

Alchemy allows us to be aware of the everyday transformations all around us and alchemists, both past and present, teach us that change is life's only constant. By thinking alchemically, we can steer that change toward bettering ourselves and the world around us.

Alchemy is the axis point for many of our modern scientific and creative fields, but it's also a religion, a pseudoscience that paved the way for chemistry, a storytelling roadmap that provides a way to think about the mind, art, and creative practice. It's why alchemy can be found at the heart of numerous, and vastly different, disciplines such as chemistry, psychology, art, and literature.

Alchemy AND Chemistry

N THE LATE MIDDLE AGES, ALCHEMY BEGAN TO UNRAVEL. Medieval rulers turned to alchemists not for their knowledge of spiritual growth but to make gold to pay off debts and fill their coffers. Official state records from Central Europe show that monarchs appointed court alchemists to make a bunch of gold to strengthen their kingdom's economy, and an obsession with gold production peaked in the 16th century. Paris, Cologne, Vienna, Prague, and other medieval cities all built laboratories for alchemists in which producing gold was the only goal. The Hapsburg Emperor Rudolf II employed numerous "gold cooks" and even worked directly with the alchemist and astronomer Tycho Brahe in alchemical laboratories built especially for Brahe.

As you might imagine, this obsession with gold reduced the true breadth of alchemy. Alchemy adepts who had apprenticed and trained so long were at odds with these alchemists who sought only to make gold for greedy royals. Nonetheless, these gold hungry alchemists employed by fancy European courts devalued all of alchemy. Europe began distrusting these gold-obsessed alchemists, derisively called "puffers," who'd often resort to trickery to convince their patrons of a successful transformation of gold. The true adepts were lumped in with the puffers without distinction, and so all of alchemy became a hack. Shakespeare contemporary Ben Jonson's 1610 comedy *The Alchemist* pokes fun at these puffers. Disapproval of puffers became so widespread that all of England got a laugh at alchemy's expense.

By the late 16th century, true alchemists who considered alchemy to be much more than a gold-making process were driven underground. Their retreat was no thanks to puffers, who created a general confusion around the philosophical principles of alchemy. Strangely enough, puffers were sometimes referred to as "chemists" and their work was known as "chemistry" or "chemystry."

An alchemist with his assistants in his laboratory.
Engraving by J. P. Le Bas after D. Teniers, late 17th to early 18th century, Paris.
A depiction of a puffer working at his furnace, trying (and undoubtedly failing) to create gold. Puffers were alchemists who only worked to create more gold for royal coffers, and soiled the true adepts of alchemy who had a more nuanced understanding.

Albert Einstein

Ever heard of Albert Einstein? Even if you have, you probably don't know all that much about Einstein as a modern alchemist, but he always held space for the unknown. Most famous for his theory of relativity, Einstein understood that time and space are relative. It's how we know that time in outer space works differently than time on Earth, especially when it comes to time's effect on light.

Alchemists' fascination with celestial bodies and the cyclical nature of time have quite a bit in common with Einstein's theory of relativity. Like Einstein, alchemists understood all things have a dual nature. In alchemy, all compounds contain some Sulfur and some Mercury; the ratio causes a compound to act in a certain way. Also like Einstein, alchemists understood light to be changeable. There's both dark light and bright light in alchemy.

Einstein's famous equation, $E = mc^2$, finds its own alchemical parallels. In addition to the two fundamental forces of the universe, Sulfur and Mercury, alchemists sometimes included Salt as a third basic component of the universe. Alchemists called the threesome the *Tria Prima*. These three fundamental compounds in alchemy can find correlations in Einstein's mass-energy equivalence equation. Mercury is energy (E). Sulfur is the speed of light (c). Salt is mass (m). Like Einstein, alchemists understood there to be a fundamental relationship between energy and mass. It's why alchemists believed First Matter was both the matter *and* raw energy of the world. Though alchemists didn't formulate this relationship into an equation like Einstein did, they understood how these three forces existed relative to one another.

In this confusion, alchemy gave way to chemistry. In its simplest terms, chemistry is physical alchemy divorced from the guiding principles of esoteric alchemy, which championed the transformation of the spiritual self and mind. As early as 1597, the German chemist and alchemist Andreas Libavius began to distinguish chemistry from alchemy in his book *Alchymia*. Robert Boyle's 1661 book, *The Sceptical Chymist*, marked the end of Aristotle's four elements and the seed of today's elements as arranged in the periodic table. It would take another hundred years or so for the French nobleman Antoine-Laurent Lavoisier to identify oxygen, in 1778, and nearly another century for the Russian chemist Dmitri Mendeleev to develop the periodic table, in 1869. Nonetheless, by the late 18th century, chemistry rose to prominence. The scientific method, research journals, and the search for new chemical compounds began to define the field of chemistry as alchemy's mystical and spiritual roots fell away.

Despite these Enlightenment chemists' best efforts to fully divorce the two fields, chemistry is still full of alchemy. Alchemists' inherent questioning and carefully written treatises are at the heart of chemistry. As is demonstrated by the detailed recipes found in Marie Meurdrac's and Isabella Cortese's books, alchemists laid the groundwork for the scientific method. Meurdrac's and Cortese's alchemical recipes were tried and true instructions that, if followed, would lead to the same perfume or healing tonic.

There's a host of alchemical equipment still used by chemists today, too, in original or modified forms. Hypatia's hydrometer, Maria Prophetissa's *tribikos*, the design for flasks and measuring equipment, and the process of cupellation, which extracted silver metal ore from lead, are all still used.

The goals of chemistry and alchemy are also linked. Just like their alchemist ancestors, chemists today are still trying to succeed in creating a modern elixir of life. It may not look like the Flamel's rough, red stone, but chemistry labs across the globe are looking for their own kind of life-extending elixirs. Chemists are constantly innovating to discover new ways to improve and extend life, from striving to improve human memory to trying to concoct the new miracle drug. Take the chemist Alexander

Fleming, who in 1928 observed how mold diminished the growth of bacteria in his Petri dish—a chemistry breakthrough that has saved many lives in the form of penicillin. While modern chemists aren't seeking one death-defying cure-all, branches of the field still look for ways to extend human life. While chemistry discoveries today might look very different from the alchemical discoveries of bygone eras, both are inspired by the same human impulse to improve and perfect human life.

Beyond chemistry, quantum physics also owes a huge debt to alchemy. The renowned 20th-century physicist Wolfgang Pauli, who coined the term "quantum physics," maintained a correspondence with Carl Jung. (Bet you didn't see that one coming!) While exchanging letters with Jung on alchemy, Pauli discovered that a physicist's state of mind could actually affect an experiment, even causing equipment to malfunction. Now, that sounds like some hardcore mental alchemy to me.

Pauli devoted his life to discovering a unified theory of everything, which has become the Great Work of modern quantum physics. Quantum physicists have already successfully captured First Matter and transmuted lead into gold. In the 1980s, nuclear scientists at the Lawrence Berkeley National Laboratory successfully transformed bismuth, an element equivalent to lead, into a (very) small amount of gold with the help of a particle accelerator and lots and lots of energy. Now quantum physicists work to understand the spiritual, unifying principle of the world—what Stephen Hawking called a "theory of everything." Concepts such as string theory abound, but proving any one of them remains tricky. It's almost as if the spiritual underpinning of alchemy needs to be rediscovered in our proof-obsessed world, allowing space for the unknown. Perhaps today's scientists could learn a thing or two from alchemists.

Alchemy AND Psychology

IKE THE AUSTRIAN-BORN PHYSICIST WOLFGANG PAULI, the Swiss psychoanalyst Carl Jung also founded a new discipline influenced by alchemy: analytical psychology. Alchemy was largely forgotten after the rise of chemistry in the late 18th century.

The complex symbolism of alchemy didn't seem so enlightened to chemists of the Enlightenment. In fact, all of those complicated symbols just made it seem as if alchemists were a bit insane and had been inhaling too many fumes. More likely, Enlightenment chemists probably didn't understand what alchemists were getting at with all their drawings of Venus and Mercury. So they threw alchemy on the trash heap of history. During the Victorian period, only occult enthusiasts, who were often obsessed with the Middle Ages, knew anything about alchemy.

By the mid-20th century, Pauli and Jung both were feeling disillusioned with their research and looked to alchemy for inspiration. Pauli, as I've mentioned, went on to become the father of quantum physics. Jung went on to found the basis of modern psychology.

Mental alchemy, as we've delved into it, is an all-inclusive term that defines how alchemists understood the mind, but alchemy also influences psychology today, largely because of Jung's work. Don't get too confused on that blurred line. Psychology is a separate scientific field devoted to the study of the human mind that, while influenced by alchemy, is not rooted in it. The distinction between mental alchemy and psychology (sometimes referred to as "psychological alchemy") is similar to the distinction that can be drawn between physical alchemy and chemistry.

So, how exactly has alchemy influenced psychology? Where to begin!

Sigmund Freud is often considered the father of modern psychology. Freud developed much of what therapy looks like today: sitting in a chair and talking problems out with a licensed therapist. But the second major figure to come along in psychology's origin story is none other than Jung. For several years, Jung followed Freud's thinking, which emphasized the importance of a patient's childhood and sexual drive in shaping their actions.

Jung ultimately broke away from Freud, believing that people are a lot more than their infant-selves and sex. He first started looking into alchemy in the 1940s, resurrecting it from history's metaphorical trashcan. Alchemy, for Jung, opened up a new way of seeing the world, paving the way for his understanding of dream analysis, personality types, the unconscious, and archetypes.

In his book *Psychology and Alchemy*, Jung discusses how a patient's dreams incorporated alchemical symbols, even though that patient knew nothing about alchemy! Jung concluded that his patient must have tapped into society's collective unconscious. Jung believed alchemists devised a collective dream with their own symbols and language, a symbology still buried in humanity's shared unconscious today.

While many in the West look toward Eastern religions such as Buddhism and Hinduism for a spiritual or mystical framework, Jung argued that alchemy acts as a far better spiritual framework because it has been an integral part of Western thought for millennia.

Like many modern psychologists, Jung believed in a basic duality of the self, a principle at the heart of alchemy. As in alchemy, Jung believed, this duality needed to be reconciled in order to achieve personal growth, or "individuation," as he put it. Jung and alchemists both believed in the importance of universal symbols, such as Mercury in alchemy or Jung's trickster. Jung referred to these persistent mental images as archetypes. Much as in the Blackening, Jung believed, personal growth could be achieved only through reckoning with your "shadow," the negative aspect of your personality, which would sometimes present itself using archetypes Jung identified. In many ways, Jung was the translator of alchemy for the 20th century, untangling its esoteric symbolism in a digestible and useful way for both psychologists and the world at large.

Jacob wrestling with the Angel *Engraving by Laplante after Gustave Dore's* The Bible in pictures. *19th century.* Jacob and the Angel represent the two sides of your personality that war with one another, the shadow/unconscious self and the known/conscious self. The two must be brought into harmony, but that's no easy task.

Psychologists continue to build upon Jung's work. When developing the Myers–Briggs personality test, the psychologists Katharine Cook Briggs and Isabel Briggs Myers looked to Jung's theories of the duality of self, which he expressed in terms of the anima/introvert (similar to Sulfur in alchemy) and animus/extrovert (Mercury in alchemy).

The collective unconscious continues to be studied not just in psychology, but also in sociology, media studies, and other fields. Jung's notions of archetypes have influenced everything from archaeology to *Star Wars*. Beyond just the field of psychology, Jung's digestible

Alchemy Applied

Jung's Alchemical Dream Analysis:

A Journal Exercise

MATERIALS

Pen or Pencil • Journal

IN THE MORNING, just when you've woken up, grab your journal, and write down anything from last night's dream you remember. Try to do so before you get out of bed and the specifics from your dream flit away from your waking mind.

IN THE EVENING, look back at what you've written about your dream, and underline or highlight anything that sticks out. A three-eyed dog? A snake in the grass?

SOMETIMES our dreams are clearly triggered by something we were thinking, reading, or watching right before we went to bed, like if you watch your favorite sitcom, and then one of the characters becomes your dream friend. Try to disregard any details that seem to have a clear origin like that. Look instead for the unusual details.

REFLECT on any alchemical symbols or metaphors from your dream. Did you meet a person with red skin? Or a dragon? Jung believed that for Westerners, alchemy loomed large in our collective unconscious.

THINK about what those specific dream details might indicate or bring up for you. You know enough about alchemy at this point to begin to analyze your dreams just like Carl Jung would have. Does the person with red skin indicate that you're on the right path and have reached the Red Phase? Does the snake indicate the cyclical sense of time, like in the alchemical symbol of the Ouroboros?

THERE'S no wrong answer here! Think about your dreams as a sort of Rorschach test where the meaning you discern is more important than any sort of "truth." (But, what is true in dreams anyhow? Have fun with it! You just might be surprised by what you uncover.)

translation of alchemy reintroduced the once forgotten art of alchemy to modern society.

Alchemy AND Literature

AGREE WITH THE WRITER PAUL KINGSNORTH—I THINK WE MISS MAGIC. We miss having the faith that our minds are powerful enough to alter the world around us.

Alchemy is a form of magic that is reliant on the belief that our minds affect real, physical change. In attempting to transform lead into gold, alchemists shaped their will to the task, and so to their realities.

Writers believe the same thing. By transforming their will into words, writers create whole other worlds for readers to exist in. When J. K. Rowling wrote *Harry Potter and the Sorceror's Stone*, she shaped her will to the story, bringing what she saw in her mind onto the page, resulting in a world that becomes all the more real in the reader's imagination.

From its beginning, alchemy has always been intertwined with writing. Thoth first gifted the knowledge of writing to the ancient Egyptians, and writing was the seed that blossomed into mathematics, alchemy, astronomy, medicine, law, philosophy, and many other disciplines. From writing, everything flowed.

Writing often creates order. It creates a reflection of ourselves on the page, a reflection that others can see themselves in. Whenever we see ourselves in a character, it shows us how interrelated we all are. It's how we know we all spring from the same source, an idea personified as First Matter or the Ouroboros. We all come from the same stuff of the universe, and ultimately we return to that source.

Norse mythology has a figure quite similar to Thoth in Odin, chief of the gods and goddesses of Asgard. In Norse mythology, Odin seeks the runes, the magical Germanic alphabet and divination tool, from the Norns, three female beings who control the course of fate. Odin hangs himself upside down from a tree, stabbing himself with his own spear as a sacrifice to the Norns. Luckily for Odin, he was a god and could survive his wounds for a while. After nine days of his self-inflicted torture, the Norns finally granted Odin the knowledge of writing. For both Norse people and ancient Egyptians, writing was the divine gift of knowledge. It was worth bleeding upside down for, at least for Odin.

Beyond writing, alchemy is present in storytelling as well. The inner journey from baseness to enlightenment through the Blackening, Whitening, and Reddening is reflected in some of our earliest stories. In the *Odyssey*, Odysseus must go through the fire of Calcination as he confronts task after harrowing task until he finally returns home to Ithaca. In the Mesopotamian *Epic of Gilgamesh*, Gilgamesh seeks a way to keep his friend Enkidu alive when the gods demand his life, only to discover that death cannot be conquered. Even in the story about Odin, he must willingly sacrifice himself in order to attain knowledge or enlightenment. Stories are all about transformation, and alchemy is the art of transformation. Inevitably, the two have intermingled.

The literature scholar Joseph Campbell spoke specifically to the relationship between stories and alchemy. Influenced by Carl Jung, Campbell believed that all myths are variations on a single, archetypal story, one he referred to as the "monomyth." In his 1949 book *The Hero With A Thousand Faces*, Campbell called this archetypal monomyth "the hero's journey." As in alchemical transformation, Campbell divided the hero's journey into three phases: departure, initiation, and return. Like in the Blackening, the departure is all about shedding your former self. The hero must leave behind what is known and accept the "call to adventure." Like in the Whitening, the initiation is where the hero embarks on a journey, embracing their identity as a hero. The hero must face "the road of trials" and finally achieve some goal of the journey (similar to the Conjunction). Then comes the Reddening, or return, where the hero returns home with the knowledge they've gained from their journey. The hero must balance their inner duality, becoming a "master of two worlds" in order to finally achieve "the freedom to live."

Campbell and alchemists both believed in the hero's journey; they just used different words to articulate it. As we've already explored, alchemists believe that all matter contains a divine, eternal essence and that they had only to purify the matter or self for that divinity to manifest.

Think again about the Ouroboros. In alchemy, we all begin and end in the same place; the only difference is the knowledge we gain along the way. Campbell's hero's journey follows the same path. The hero must not only begin and end in the same place, but also realize they've had the power to do so within them all along.

Campbell's theories went on to influence filmmakers, writers, and storytellers of all media. When developing *Star Wars*, George Lucas wanted to create a modern myth, and he used the archetypes Campbell identified in his story of Luke Skywalker. Campbell's theories have been applied to everything from *Jane Eyre* and *Moby Dick* to Stephen King and Disney.

Cut to the heart of storytelling and writing, and you'll find the lively beating heart of alchemy. From ancient Egypt to Norse mythology, writing, magic, and alchemy have always been intertwined, because all three orbit around the art of transformation.

Alchemy AND Art

THE HISTORY OF ART AND ALCHEMY IS A LONG ONE. The achievements of physical alchemy propelled art making to take new forms. In their many experiments, alchemists developed compounds and processes used by artists of the past and present. Alchemy helped develop everything from oil paints, metal alloys for sculpture, glassmaking techniques, and chemicals used in developing photography.

As with many disciplines before the age of Enlightenment, there was a huge amount of crossover between alchemy and the arts. Freed from the sometimes rigid distinctions we draw today, many alchemists were also artists, and many artists were also alchemists. The Flemish painter Jan Van Eyck was described by fellow painter Giorgio Vasari as "a man who delighted in alchemy." Van Eyck was constantly experimenting in his laboratory, using alchemical techniques to create the perfect mixture of oil and pigment for his paints. In fact, Van Eyck improved oil painting so much that he's often mistakenly cited as the inventor of oil paints.

Romanticism and a Look at Mary Shelley

Numerous writers found inspiration from alchemy, especially Romantics such as Samuel Taylor Coleridge, John Keats, and Mary Shelley (shown at center).

Shortly before she began writing *Frankenstein, or the Modern Prometheus*, Mary Shelley visited Castle Frankenstein, where the famed alchemist Conrad Dippel had worked. Local legends even claim that Dippel experimented upon human cadavers, not unlike Shelley's protagonist, Doctor Frankenstein. It's possible that Shelley heard the legend and not only borrowed the name "Frankenstein" for her protagonist but took inspiration from these grisly castle legends.

The themes in Shelley's *Frankenstein* share her fellow Romantics alchemical roots. Shelley's *Frankenstein* strives to reconcile the distance between chemistry and the sublime/spiritual, a preoccupation shared by alchemists. As the scholar Elizabeth Brocious points out, Frankenstein's monster elicits terror in his creator to such a degree that it moves Doctor Frankenstein toward "a higher self-knowledge."

Just as the physical transmutation of lead into gold was supposed to create a "golden" self, Frankenstein's creature enlightens its maker, though in a very different manner. While the alchemists' experiments created higher forms of matter, Frankenstein's work creates a horrific monster. Frankenstein's creature enlightens the doctor, but it does so through a combination of horror and awe, turning alchemy on its head, with enlightenment transmuted into enduring literary horror.

Like Van Eyck, the painter and inventor Leonardo da Vinci also experimented with alchemy. Leonardo's mentor, the Italian goldsmith, sculptor, and painter Andrea del Verrocchio, was a known alchemist. Leonardo himself was hesitant to embrace the title of alchemist, since puffers had already discredited alchemy by his time. Nonetheless, his private journals contain multiple entries about alchemical experiments. Some of the entries mention the mixing of compounds referred to as Mercury, Venus, and Jupiter. It doesn't get more alchemical than referring to metals by their planetary associations. Leonardo even writes about Hermes Trismigistus, the medieval name given to Thoth. The scholars Lynn Picknett and Clive Prince write in their book *Turin Shroud* that it's likely Leonardo used his knowledge of alchemy to create the holy Shroud of Turin, Jesus's supposed burial cloth bearing an imprint of his face, which they posit could be the world's first photograph.

Beyond physical alchemy and experimentation, alchemy's rich symbolic language inspired many medieval and Renaissance artists. In addition to mentoring Leonardo da Vinci, Andrea del Verrocchio also instructed a young Sandro Filipepi, better known as the painter Botticelli, who later incorporated all sorts of alchemical symbols into his paintings.

In Botticelli's "Primavera," the goddess Flora, bedecked in flowers, has a violet—a flower associated with the Red Phase and the duality between life and death that occurs during alchemy's last phase—centrally placed on her forehead. Just beside Flora is the nymph Chloris, who transforms into the goddess Flora after marrying the March wind, Zephyrus. Botticelli depicts the transformation of Chloris to Flora, and just in case you miss it, he uses the violet on Flora's forehead to symbolize the life of Flora brought about by the death of Chloris.

Alchemy's rich symbolism inspired plenty of other Renaissance artists, including Bellini, Titian, Giorgione, and Bosch. The famed German artist Albrecht Dürer illustrated the Egyptian alchemical text *Hieroglyphica*, depicting the sun, the moon, and a basilisk. Remember, in alchemy, the sun and moon represent the two fundamental forces of the world: Mercury (the Sun) and Sulfur (the Moon). The basilisk is indicative of the Ouroboros, and the eternal, cyclical nature of matter and time.

Alchemists used a rich language of symbols to encode their experiments. Some beautiful alchemical manuscripts, such as the late 14th-century *Aurora consurgens*, are full of images of hermaphrodites and the Sacred Marriage. The importance of symbols in alchemical manuscripts inspired the artists not only of the Renaissance but of later periods as well.

Alchemy fascinated the late 18th-century poet and artist William Blake (1757–1827). Both Paracelsus and Jakob Böhme, the mystic and alchemist, were mentors and friends of Blake's. Blake believed that every era in history gained power through the renewed study of alchemy. In fact, Blake's own interest in alchemy went on to inspire the Romantics of the 19th century, such as Mary Shelley.

Blake's poetry and paintings are full of alchemical symbols. In his book *The Marriage of Heaven and Hell*, an angel transforms before the Devil, becoming blue, then yellow, and then white-pink, mirroring the colors present during alchemical experiments: black/blue, yellow, white, and

Basilisk
In alchemy, the Basilisk embodies the bringing together of dualities with its rooster head and reptilian tail. It is also sometimes an alternative depiction of the Alchemical Dragon.

red. Blake's last and longest prophetic book, *Jerusalem: The Emanation of the Giant Albion*, is chock-full of alchemical symbolism. In chapter 1, the character Los works tirelessly at his furnace to divide male and female. In the final chapter, all things become both real and unreal as everything is united in the Divine Body, like in Coagulation.

Alchemy continues to inspire more contemporary artists as well. The Los Angeles-based artist Christopher Ulrich's surrealist paintings include "The Alchemist," and he designed an oven hood featuring images inspired from medieval alchemical texts such as Michael Maier's 1617 *Atalanta Fugiens*. The Chicago-based artist Karena Karras has crafted paintings that feature the Blackening, furnaces, and other alchemical symbols. Her inspiration springs from Jung, alchemy, and surrealist painters such as Salvador Dalí, who were in turn inspired by alchemy's rich symbology.

Art making is always about transformation. Regardless of if you're transforming a canvas, a story, or your mind, we are standing in the alchemist's shadow as we toil away at transforming the world around us and ourselves for the better.

CONCLUSION

Embracing ᴛʜᴇ Alchemist Within

CONGRATULATIONS ARE IN ORDER. Congratulations, dear friend, on finishing this leg of your alchemical journey, and look at all you've learned! You know about Thoth and alchemy's ancient Egyptian roots. You know about the three main branches of alchemy. You've waded through the four elements and their role in alchemical transformation. You understand what the Great Work is and alchemy's role in the even greater cosmos. And, you know the ways in which alchemy and its principles have come to inform everything from quantum physics to *Star Wars*. We forget that finishing a book is an accomplishment to be lauded, too, so well done, friend. Give yourself a pat on the back.

When I first learned about alchemy from Deborah Harkness's *A Discovery of Witches*, it took a long time before I could even venture to define alchemy. Alchemy, with its beautiful, esoteric medieval manuscripts and hermetic origins, likes to defy explanation. It's my hope that with the help of this book, you are off to a much clearer start.

But allow me to assure you, there's a lot more to learn. From Jung's writings to those of the Chinese alchemist Ge Hong, alchemy encompasses several millennia of human knowledge, and it has left behind a treasure trove of secrets. Whatever sparked your interest in these pages—whether that's the Ouroboros or the Flamels—let that curiosity propel you into your next alchemical adventure.

Studying and writing about alchemy serves to remind me of reality's intricate web. Wolfgang Pauli and Carl Jung both looked to alchemy when contemporary research and study left them uninspired. We can gain so much by looking at the wisdom of the ancient alchemists. Who knows? Maybe we'll create new disciplines, like Pauli or Jung, or adopt a more nuanced way to see the world around us and its transformations.

Long before scientists' explored string theory or atoms, alchemists understood intuitively that the world shares the same basic matter. They understood the inherent duality and divinity of everything. It's a beautiful and true way to look at the world around us—one we could all stand to adopt.

Too often we forget how quickly the world changes, and our lives with it. Alchemists harnessed that ever-present change to transform the world, their minds, and even their souls and spirits. Alchemists marveled at the universe, mixed potions, and worked toward bettering themselves. I think our contemporary world is missing some of the alchemists' wonder and curiosity. So, go forth, dear alchemists, and wonder. Be curious. Harness this ever-changing world of ours!

RESOURCES

Books

Alchemy & Mysticism by Alexander Roob
The art history scholar Alexander Roob compiled the most comprehensive guide to alchemical images and paintings. It's a bit dense, but the high-quality color images make it totally worthwhile. Produced by the Hermetic Museum.

Astrology, Magic, and Alchemy in Art by Matilde Battistini
This beautiful book written by the art critic Matilde Battistini is a great, digestible resource that's easy to flip through to specific entries. It's an especially great resource for an in-depth description of each planet in the Ladder of the Planets.

The Chemical Choir: A History of Alchemy by P. G. Maxwell-Stuart
For the history nerds out there, the historian P. G. Maxwell-Stuart has written a comprehensive history of alchemy from its beginnings to the 20th century.

The Emerald Tablet: Alchemy for Personal Transformation
by Dennis William Hauck
An approachable guide that explains how to apply the ancient teachings of *The Emerald Tablet* to personal transformation.

The Encyclopedia of Magic and Alchemy by Rosemary Guiley
The best alchemy encyclopedia out there. Rosemary Guiley's writing is well researched and easy to understand.

The Secrets of Alchemy by Lawrence M. Principe
The historian and leading authority on alchemy Lawrence M. Principe's book is a scholarly look at alchemy's history and its impact on modern society. Principe even includes a couple of the recipes for some of the most famous alchemical experiments he's decoded, including the "glass of antimony" and "philosophers' tree."

Websites

AlchemyLab.com

Probably the best online resource for alchemy, this site is an approach-able, user-friendly resource with a dictionary of alchemical terms, historical overview, and even more books to check out. Be sure to explore the Lunar and Solar Path portals on the home page.

AlchemyStudy.com

If you want to dive further into alchemy through an online course, this wonderful site offers several modules to choose from, all taught by International Alchemy Guild–certified alchemists.

Levity.com/alchemy

This site has everything: full texts of alchemical manuscripts, images, history, and even alchemical poetry.

TheGreatCourses.com/professors/lawrence-m-principe

If you liked *The Secrets of Alchemy* or just prefer a course format, check out Lawrence M. Principe's Great Courses modules, "Science and Religion" and "History of Science: Antiquity to 1700." The Great Courses is a phenomenal resource for learning more about any subject.

Guilds and Institutional Resources

The International Alchemy Guild (IAG)

Founded in the 1970s but tracing its roots back to the 16th-century Austrian alchemist Wilhelm von Rosenberg, the International Alchemy Guild hosts events, publishes newsletters and articles, and is affiliated with *AlchemyStudy.com* to further the teachings of alchemy today. Membership to the guild costs $40 for a year and $95 for three years (students pay only $50 for three years).

California Institute of Integral Studies (CIIS)

A private, nonprofit university founded in 1968, CIIS offers undergraduate, graduate, and online courses that explore psychology, philosophy, religion, women's spirituality, cultural anthropology, and more.

Miscellany

The "Alchemy and Art" episode on the Art History Babes *podcast*
Recorded with the contemporary artist and alchemist Faith Sponsler,
this podcast is a fun, informative first step into the world of alchemy
specifically from an art history perspective.

REFERENCES

All references are organized by chapter according to the order sources were used in the text. In other words, the references are organized chronologically rather than alphabetically.

Chapter 1: What Is Alchemy?

Ogilvy, Guy. *The Great Wizards of Antiquity: The Dawn of Western Magic and Alchemy*. Woodbury, MN: Llewellyn Publications, 2019.

Raven, Maarten J. *Egyptian Magic: The Quest for Thoth's Book of Secrets*. Cairo: American University in Cairo Press, 2012.

Kelly, Jack. *Gunpowder: A History of the Explosive That Changed the World*. London: Atlantic, 2005.

Principe, Lawrence. *The Secrets of Alchemy*. University of Chicago Press, 2013.

Holmyard, Eric John. *Alchemy*. Harmondsworth, UK: Penguin Books, 1957.

Haeffner, Mark. *Dictionary of Alchemy*. London: Aeon Books, 2015.

Sella, Andrea. "Classic Kit: Mary's Bath." Chemistry World, June 29, 2009. chemistryworld.com/opinion/classic-kit-marys-bath/3004925.article.

Guarino, Ben. "This Chemist Is Unlocking the Secrets of Alchemy." *Washington Post*, January 30, 2018. washingtonpost.com/news /speaking-of-science/wp/2018/01/30/this-chemist-is-unlocking -the-secrets-of-alchemy.

International Alchemy Guild. "About the Guild." Accessed December 8, 2019. alchemyguild.memberlodge.org/page-752209.

Andrea. "Moon-Based Herbal Medicine Making: How to Make an Herbal Tincture with the Lunar Cycle." Frugally Sustainable, January 8, 2019. frugallysustainable.com/moon-based-herbal-medicine-making-how -to-make-an-herbal-tincture-with-the-lunar-cycle.

———. "How to Make and Use Lavender Flower Extract." Frugally Sustainable, January 9, 2019. frugallysustainable.com/how-to-make-and-use-lavender-flower-extract.

Roob, Alexander. *"Alchemy & Mysticism.* Cologne: Taschen, 2019.

Regardie, Israel. *Gold: Israel Regardie's Lost Book of Alchemy.* Woodbury, MN: Llewellyn Publications, 2015.

Hoeller, Stephan A. "C. G. Jung and the Alchemical Renewal." The Gnosis Archive, 1988. gnosis.org/jung_alchemy.htm.

Cetta, Matthew. "Photogenic Alchemy." Accessed December 8, 2019. matthewcetta.com/portfolios/photogenic-alchemy.

Campbell, Joseph. *The Hero with a Thousand Faces.* London: Fontana Press, 1993.

Chapter 2: Alchemy and The Elements

Roob, Alexander. *Alchemy & Mysticism.* Cologne: Taschen, 2019.

Sioura, Thomi. "Hippocrates: The Four Elements of Nature in the Human Body." Mentora. September 13, 2018. mentora.gr/hippocrates-the-elements-of-nature-in-the-human-body.

Haeffner, Mark. *Dictionary of Alchemy.* London: Aeon Books, 2015.

Cheney, Liana De Girolami. "Lavinia Fontana's Cleopatra the Alchemist." *Journal of Literature and Art Studies* 8, no. 8 (2018). doi.org/10.17265/2159-5836/2018.08.004.

Taylor, F. Sherwood. "The Origins of Greek Alchemy." *Ambix* 1, no. 1 (1937): 43. doi.org/10.1179/000269837790223499.

Alic, Margaret. "Women and Technology in Ancient Alexandria: Maria and Hypatia." *Women's Studies International Quarterly* 4, no. 3 (1981): 305–12. doi.org/10.1016/s0148-0685(81)96493-9.

Ogilvy, Guy. *The Great Wizards of Antiquity: The Dawn of Western Magic and Alchemy.* Woodbury, MN: Llewellyn Publications, 2019.

Kirk, Geoffrey Stephen, J. E. Raven, and Malcolm Schofield. *The Presocratic Philosophers*. Cambridge, UK: Cambridge University Press, 1993.

Guiley, Rosemary Ellen. *The Encyclopedia of Magic and Alchemy*. New York: Facts on File, 2006.

Ray, Meredith K. *Daughters of Alchemy: Women and Scientific Culture in Early Modern Italy*. Cambridge, MA: Harvard University Press, 2015.

Ogilvie, Marilyn, and Joy Harvey, eds. *The Biographical Dictionary of Women in Science: Pioneering Lives from Ancient Times to the Mid-20th Century*. New York: Routledge, 2000.

Gordon, Robin L. *Searching for the Soror Mystica: The Lives and Science of Women Alchemists*. Lanham, MD: University Press of America, 2013.

Åkerman Susanna. *Queen Christina of Sweden and Her Circle: The Transformation of a Seventeenth-Century Philosophical Libertine*. Leiden, Netherlands: Brill, 1991.

Chapter 3: The Great Work of Alchemy

Ecclesiastes. *Holy Bible: Containing the Old and New Testaments: King James Version*. New York: American Bible Society, 2010.

Pleij, Herman. *Colors Demonic and Divine: Shades of Meaning in the Middle Ages and After*. New York: Columbia University Press, 2005.

Humburg, Burt. "On the Color Changes in the 'Great Work,' or the Alchemical Transformation of Matter." Alchemy. Accessed December 10, 2019. alchemywebsite.com/humburg.html.

Bright, Bonnie. "An Alchemical Take on the Film *Black Swan*." Depth Psychology Alliance. Accessed December 9, 2019. api.ning.com /files/T*7R11QNcS6cVmLqJrlFdKE8QPvQCNQzrS9VpWRDa0YGU 63tOrmooohtZYr0M5jP8ohkXIesx3OW8Us9l70hHCz1VoR4rWjd /AlchemicalTakeonBlackSwanBBright.pdf.

Franz, Marie-Luise von. *Alchemy: An Introduction to the Symbolism and the Psychology*. Toronto: Inner City Books, 1980.

Hard, Robin, and H. J. Rose. *The Routledge Handbook of Greek Mythology: Based on H. J. Rose's Handbook of Greek Mythology*. London: Routledge, 2004.

Hauck, Dennis William. *The Emerald Tablet: Alchemy for Personal Transformation*. New York: Penguin/Arkana, 1999.

Odorisio, David M. "Of Gods and Stones: Alchemy, Jung, and the Dark Night of St. John of the Cross." *Journal of Transpersonal Psychology* 47, no. 1 (January 1, 2015).

Ritner, Robert K. "Innovations and Adaptations in Ancient Egyptian Medicine." *Journal of Near Eastern Studies* 59, no. 2 (2000): 107–17. doi.org/10.1086/468799.

Dawson, Warren. "A Strange Drug." *Aegyptus* 12 (1932): 12–15.

Hauck, Dennis William. "The Seven Operations of Alchemy." The AZoth Ritual. Accessed December 10, 2019. azothalchemy.org/azoth_ritual.htm.

Stratford, Jordan. *"A Dictionary of Western Alchemy*. Wheaton, IL: Quest Books, 2011.

Rank, Scott. "Little Known Links Between Spirits You Drink and the Holy Spirit." Ancient Origins. July 7, 2017. ancient-origins.net/history -ancient-traditions/little-known-links-between-spirits-you-drink -and-holy-spirit-008365.

Hallum, B. C. "The Tome of Images: an Arabic Compilation of Texts by Zosimos of Panopolis and a Source of The Turba Philosophorum." *Ambix* 56, no. 1 (2009): 76–88. doi.org/10.1179/174582309x405255.

Dickson, Donald R. "The Alchemistical Wife: The Identity of Thomas Vaughan's 'Rebecca.'" *The Seventeenth Century* 13, no. 1 (1998): 36–49. doi.org/10.1080/0268117x.1998.10555440.

Haeffner, Mark. *Dictionary of Alchemy*. London: Aeon Books, 2015.

Avens, Cynthia. "Sacred Marriage Combining the Divine Feminine and Divine Masculine." Christosophia. Accessed December 10, 2019. christosophia.org/essaysthesacredmarriage.html.

Mathers, Dale. *Alchemy and Psychotherapy: Post-Jungian Perspectives.* London: Routledge, Taylor & Francis Group, 2014.

Ogilvy, Guy. *The Great Wizards of Antiquity: The Dawn of Western Magic and Alchemy.* Woodbury, MN: Llewellyn Publications, 2019

Chapter 4: Alchemy and The Planets

Stephenson, F. R., K. K. C. Yau, and H. Hunger. "Records of Halley's Comet on Babylonian Tablets." *Nature* 314, no. 6012 (1985): 587–92. doi.org/10.1038/314587a0.

Almirantis, Yannis. "The Paradox of the Planetary Metals." *Journal of Scientific Exploration* 19, no. 1 (2005): 31–42.

Battistini, Matilde. *Astrology, Magic, and Alchemy in Art*, 14–86. Los Angeles: J. Paul Getty Museum, 2007.

W., Hewitt William. *Astrology for Beginners: An Easy Guide To Understanding and Interpreting Your Chart.* Woodbury, MN: Llewellyn, 2016.

Pearson, Nicholas. *Stones of the Goddess: Crystals for the Divine Feminine.* Rochester, VT: Inner Traditions, 2019.

Stratford, Jordan. *A Dictionary of Western Alchemy*, 10. Wheaton, IL: Quest Books, 2011.

European Southern Observatory. "Mercury's Orbit and Visibility." May 7, 2003. eso.org/public/outreach/eduoff/vt-2004/mt-2003/mt-mercury -orbit.html.

Wright, David Curtis. *The History of China.* Westport, CT: Greenwood Press, 2001.

DiBernard, Barbara. *Alchemy and* Finnegans Wake. Albany: State University of New York Press, 1980.

Lide, David R. *CRC Handbook of Chemistry and Physics: A Ready-Reference Book of Chemical and Physical Data.* Boca Raton, FL: CRC Press, 2004.

Sutherland, Carol Humphrey Vivian. *Gold: Its Beauty, Power, and Allure.* London: Thames and Hudson, 1969.

Bernstein, Peter L. *The Power of Gold: The History of an Obsession,* 3. Hoboken, NJ: John Wiley & Sons, 2012.

"Artemis: Greek Goddess of Hunting & Wild Animals." Theoi Greek Mythology. Accessed December 10, 2019. theoi.com/olympios /artemis.html.

Chapter 5: The Axis of Alchemy

Paneth, Fritz. "Ancient and Modern Alchemy." *Science* 64, no. 1661 (1926): 410. doi.org/10.1126/science.64.1661.409.

Guiley, Rosemary Ellen. *The Encyclopedia of Magic and Alchemy.* New York: Facts on File, 2006.

"Andreas Libavius—Scientist of the Day." Linda Hall Library, July 18, 2019. lindahall.org/andreas-libavius.

"From Alchemy to Chemistry." Khan Academy. Accessed December 10, 2019. khanacademy.org/partner-content/big-history-project/stars -and-elements/other-material3/a/from-alchemy-to-chemistry.

Lorch, Mark. "5 Chemistry Breakthroughs That Shaped Our Modern World." *Discover Magazine.* June 2, 2015. discovermagazine.com/the-sciences /5-chemistry-breakthroughs-that-shaped-our-modern-world.

Matson, John. "Fact or Fiction?: Lead Can Be Turned into Gold." *Scientific American.* January 31, 2014. scientificamerican.com/article/fact-or -fiction-lead-can-be-turned-into-gold.

Rosen, Steven M. "Pauli's Dream: Jung, Modern Physics, and Alchemy." *Quadrant* 44, no. 2 (2014): 49–71.

Waude, Adam. "How Carl Jung's Archetypes and Collective Consciousness Affect Our Psyche." Psychologist World, January 22, 2016.
psychologistworld.com/cognitive/carl-jung-analytical-psychology.

Kingsnorth, Paul. "The Great Work: Alchemy and the Power of Words."
Emergence Magazine. Accessed December 10, 2019. emergencemagazine
.org/story/the-great-work.

McCoy, Daniel. "Odin's Discovery of the Runes." Norse Mythology for
Smart People. Accessed December 10, 2019. norse-mythology.org/tales
/odins-discovery-of-the-runes.

Brocious, Elizabeth Olsen. "Transcendental Exchange: Alchemical Dis-
course in Romantic Philosophy and Literature." 2008. scholarsarchive
.byu.edu/cgi/viewcontent.cgi?article=2339&context=etd.

Florescu, Radu. *In Search of Frankenstein: Exploring the Myths behind
Mary Shelley's Monster.* London: Robson, 1999.

"The Art of Alchemy." Getty Research Institute. Accessed December 10,
2019. getty.edu/research/exhibitions_events/exhibitions/alchemy.

"Art and Alchemy." Max Planck Institute for the History of Science.
Accessed December 10, 2019. mpiwg-berlin.mpg.de/research/projects
/FGDupre_Dupre_Nelson_Alchemy.

Daly, Jonathan W. *How Europe Made the Modern World: Creating the Great
Divergence.* London: Bloomsbury Academic, 2020.

Emerys, Chevalier. *Revelation of the Holy Grail: Bringing to Light the
Secrets of the Knights Templar, Rosicrucians, Freemasons, the Ark of the
Covenant, Rennes-Le Château, Atlantis, and Alchemy.* Self-published, 2007.

Berry, Philippa. "The Voice of the Daemon: Inspiration and the Poetic
Arts in Boticelli's 'Primavera.'" *Poimavers De La Voix* 7 (2005): 13–26.
journals.openedition.org/sillagescritiques/1018?lang=en.

Dürer, Albrecht. *Drawing of the Sun, the Moon and a Basilisk*. British Museum. Accessed December 10, 2019. research.britishmuseum.org /research/collection_online/collection_object_details.aspx?objectId =720585&partId=1.

Roberts, Maureen B. "'Ethereal Chemicals': Alchemy and the Romantic Imagination." *Romanticism on the Net*, no. 5 (February 1997). doi.org /10.7202/005734ar.

Roob, Alexander. *Alchemy & Mysticism*. Cologne: Taschen, 2019.

Black, Joseph, Leonard Conolly, Kate Flint, Isobel Grundy, Roy Liuzza, Jerome McGann, Anne Prescott, Barry Qualls, and Claire Waters. *The Broadview Anthology of Romantic Poetry*. Peterborough, Ontario, Canada: Broadview Press, 2016.

Grossman, Pam. "Interview with Karena Karras." Phantasmaphile, January 6, 2007. phantasmaphile.com/2007/01/interview_with_.html.

GLOSSARY

ADEPT: A master of alchemy; someone who knows all of alchemy's secrets

ALCHEMICAL CHILD: The new substance created during the Conjunction, symbolically understood to be the hermaphrodite child of the Sacred Marriage between the Red King and White Queen; also known as the philosopher's child, *adrogyne*, or *rebis*

ALCHEMICAL DRAGON: The raw energy of the world necessary for transformation, associated with a mysterious, indefinable substance known as philosophical mercury (different from your run-of-the-mill mercury, or quicksilver)

ALCHEMY: The art of transformation, both in the laboratory and within oneself

ADROGYNE: An alchemical depiction of a hermaphrodite representing the union of opposites in the Conjunction

ALEMBIC: Or *stillhead*, vessel that allows alchemists to purify substances during Distillation and Dissolution

ARTISTIC ALCHEMY: Where art and alchemy meet; using alchemical concepts and methods in the production of art

BLACK PHASE: Also known as the Blackening, or *Nigredo*, it's the first phase of the Great Work, where the impurities of the spiritual self, mind, and matter are identified; considered the most time-intensive phase of the Great Work

CALCINATION: The first stage of the Seven Stages of Alchemy and part of the Black Phase, where a substance is burned over a flame or with a "liquid fire," such as an acid or corrosive chemical, until it is reduced to ashes; the word itself means "reduced to bone by burning"

CLIMBING THE LADDER OF THE PLANETS: A way to conceptualize the Great Work, climbing the Ladder of the Planets meant climbing toward physical and metaphysical perfection, because each of the seven ruling planets (Saturn, Jupiter, Mars, Venus, Mercury, Moon, and Sun) corresponded with the Seven Stages of alchemical transformation

COAGULATION: The final stage of the Seven Stages of Alchemy and the part of the Red Phase where the essence refined in Distillation is solidified; when the child of Conjunction is born, and all this work takes form both physically and metaphysically; the moment when the body becomes metaphysical and the spirit and mind take on a body; the result of a successful Coagulation is the Philosopher's Stone

COLLECTIVE UNCONSCIOUS: Jung's notion that we all share a subconscious derived from ancestral memory—it's how his patients, with no knowledge of alchemy, could have dreams with specific alchemical symbols

CONJUNCTION: The fourth stage of the Seven Stages of Alchemy and the part of the White Phase where the purified matter from Separation creates an altogether new substance, known as the Child of the Conjunction, the alchemical child, or *rebis* (Latin for "double-thing"); also known as *conjunctio*

DISSOLUTION: (sometimes called *solution*) The second stage of the Seven Stages of Alchemy and the part of the Black Phase where the ashes from Calcination are dissolved in a liquid solvent

DISTILLATION: The sixth stage of the Seven Stages of Alchemy and the part of the Red Phase where the matter is further purified through evaporation or *cohobation* (repeatedly purifying a substance in liquid)

EMERALD TABLET: Ancient legendary tablet with Thoth's esoteric teachings, thought to be housed in the Library of Alexandria before its destruction; the oldest known mention of the *Tablet* dates back to the sixth century, in the Arabic *Book of Balinas the Wise on Causes*

ESOTERIC ALCHEMY: Inner alchemy, encompassing both mental and especially spiritual alchemy

EXOTERIC ALCHEMY: Another name for physical alchemy

FERMENTATION: The fifth stage of the Seven Stages of Alchemy and the part of the Red Phase where the "child" from Conjunction is matured with fermenting bacteria over a low, controlled heat (unlike the direct flames of Calcination)

FIRST MATTER: The chaotic, raw energy of the world and the essential matter of all things; also known as *Prima Materia*

FLAMELS: The 14th-century alchemists Nicolas and Perenelle, who are believed to have created the Philosopher's Stone

GREAT WORK: The alchemical work of purifying and refining any material into its highest form through the Seven Stages; also known as *Magnum Opus*

HYPATIA: (370–415 CE) The Alexandrian alchemist who improved upon Kleopatra's alembic and invented a device to measure water levels as well as a graduated hydroscope or hydrometer, which could measure the gravity of a liquid

JABIR IBN HAYYAN: (722/723–815 CE) or Geber, as he was known in medieval Europe, was an Arab alchemist and the first to posit that metals were created depending on their ratio of Sulfur to Mercury, and their purity

KLEOPATRA: A third-century-CE Alexandrian alchemist who invented the alembic, or stillhead

LUNA: Another name for the Moon, the penultimate planet in the Ladder of the Planets, associated with the White Queen

MARIA PROPHETISSA: (also known as "Mary the Jewess") A third-century-CE Alexandrian alchemist who invented the *tribikos*

MENTAL ALCHEMY: The transformation of the mind through alchemical principles as first conceptualized by the Swiss psychoanalyst Carl Jung

MERCURY: One of two fundamental forces of the universe, opposite sulfur; as first put forward by Jabir, alchemists believed that all matter contained sulfur and mercury, and that the purest of substances (such as gold) contained a perfect balance of the two; Mercury is usually equated with the striving energy of the Red King

ONE MIND: The essence or energy of the universe in alchemy

OUROBOROS: Alchemical symbol of how energy is neither created nor destroyed but only transformed; depicted by a dragon or serpent devouring its own tail

PARACELSUS: Nickname for Renaissance alchemist Theophrastus Philippus Aurelius Bombastus von Hohenheim, who used the elements to transform the field of medicine

PHILOSOPHER'S STONE: The result of the Seven Stages and the Great Work that could transform anything into its supreme, "golden" form; the universal solvent and the elixir of life

PHILOSOPHICAL MERCURY: Associated with the Alchemical Dragon, it's the raw energy of the world; not to be confused with actual quicksilver, or mercury

PHYSICAL ALCHEMY: The transformation of actual substances using the elements: air, fire, water, and earth; the lab-based experiments in alchemy; also known as exoteric alchemy

PUFFERS: A derogatory name applied to alchemists in the late medieval period who were only after gold and often weren't true adepts

PUTREFACTION: The natural decay of a substance after the Blackening and Whitening instigate the fermentation process, sometimes producing a rainbow of brilliant colors called the Peacock's Tail

PSYCHOLOGICAL ALCHEMY: The way the principles of alchemy continue to influence the field of psychology

QUICKSILVER: Another name for physical mercury (you know, the one that made hatters go mad)

QUINTESSENCE: Similar to Aristotle's fifth element, Ether, Quintessence is the building block of the heavens or divine realm and the spark of some higher power; fundamentally unknowable

RED KING: Alchemical symbol associated with the striving energy of the spirit, the Red Phase, and Sulfur; thought to be active, fiery, and energetic

RED PHASE: The last phase of alchemical transformation, where the Philosopher's Stone is achieved, encompassing Fermentation, Distillation, and Coagulation; also known as the Reddening and by the Latin *Rubedo*

SACRED MARRIAGE: The union of the Red King and White Queen during Conjunction

SALT: Any rigid form—in physical alchemy, a Salt is a solid; in mental alchemy, Salt is our limited understanding of who we are

SEPARATION: The third stage of the Seven Stages of Alchemy and the part of the White Phase where the substance from the Black Phase is filtered to retrieve its essential parts; also known as *separatio*

SEVEN STAGES OF ALCHEMY: The seven stages necessary for any alchemical transformation, physical, spiritual or mental—Calcination, Dissolution, Separation, Conjunction, Fermentation, Distillation, and Coagulation

SOCIAL ALCHEMY: A form of alchemy rooted in the transformation of relationships; encompasses both personal relationship transformation (between friends or lovers) and societal transformation (such as ending poverty or slavery)

SOL: Another name for the Sun, the final planet in the Ladder of the Planets, associated with the Red King

SOUL: The contented, present aspect of the spiritual self associated with the White Queen; also known as *animus*

SPIRITUAL ALCHEMY: The transformation of the spiritual self (both soul and spirit) through alchemical principles; also known as esoteric alchemy

SPIRIT: The striving, energetic aspect of the spiritual self that seeks self-improvement, associated with the Red King; also known as *spiritus*

SULFUR: One of two fundamental forces of the universe, opposite mercury; first put forward by Jabir, alchemists believed that all matter contained both sulfur and mercury, and that the purest substances (such as gold) contained a perfect balance of the two; sulfur is usually equated with passivity, contentment, and the White Queen

THOTH: Egyptian god of writing considered the father of many disciplines, including alchemy, mathematics, agriculture, medicine, religion, magic, and others; usually depicted as a man with the head of an ibis (a tall Egyptian wading bird) who is carrying a tablet; known as Hermes to the Greeks and Hermes Trismegistus, or "thrice-great Hermes," to medievals

TRANSMUTATION: Fancy alchemical word for transformation, especially relating to metals.

TRIA PRIMA: The three basic components of the universe—Sulfur, Mercury, and Salt

TRIBIKOS: A double-walled container that aids in the collection and distillation of heated substances; still used today; invented by Maria Prophetissa

ULTIMA MATERIA: Latin for the ultimate material, when the matter produces a halo or aura of light. The *Ultima materia* is the mental and spiritual Philosopher's Stone.

WHITE PHASE: Also known as the Whitening, or *Albedo,* the second phase of the Great Work, where pure matter is separated from its impurities and transformed into a new compound

WHITE QUEEN: Alchemical symbol associated with the contented energy of the soul, the White Phase, and Mercury; thought to be watery, passive, settled

YELLOWING: A fourth phase of the Great Work sometimes inserted between the White and Red phases; referred to a moment when the appearance of the matter became yellow or golden in color, indicating that the alchemist was on the right track to turn a base metal into gold; also known as the Yellow Phase, *citrinas,* or *xanthosis*

ZOSIMOS OF PANOPOLIS: An alchemist and Gnostic mystic who lived at the end of the third and beginning of the fourth centuries CE; he wrote about the transformation of lead into gold as the Great Work in physical alchemy, and he worked with his student, Theosebeia, to achieve that transformation in the laboratory; the first alchemist to really define the Great Work in terms of the purification of the spiritual self

INDEX

ACKNOWLEDGMENTS

To Momma. Thank you for believing I could do this before I did. To Dad, for always saying you're proud of me and bragging to your friends about your author daughter. To Chazin, for distracting me with roommate sagas and *The Office* references. For Broha, this one's for your nerdy side I wish we had had more time to talk about. To Mom (Em), for your encouragement and always reminding me where home is. To Big Sar, Uncle Chris, Aunt Trish, Aunt Beth, Aunt Jill, Uncle Bill, my Uncle Michaels (x2). To Wendy, Nick, Mitchell, and the whole Mader/Berry/Gase crew. To Katie, Annabeth, Chris, Simon, Sam, and Jack. To Ray, Grandma, Grandpa, and Uncle Joe—I know you all would've loved this. I'm so lucky to call you family. I love you all so much.

To my editor, Jesse Aylen, for all the encouraging comments (I saved every last one). This book wouldn't exist without you. To Susan Haynes and the whole Callisto crew. Thank you for inviting me into the fold. I feel so incredibly grateful to be counted among your authors.

To Marina Galperina and the team at Gizmodo, who published my first article on alchemy. Y'all rock my nerdy, medieval socks!

To all the mentors and teachers from my school days. To Scott Korb. Thank you for fielding my questions and telling me to go for it. To the professors who inspired and fostered my fascination in all things medieval:

Dr. Mo Pareles, Dr. Andrew Romig, Dr. Martha Dana Rust. To Dr. Cyd Cipolla, Ben Steinfeld, Kris Diaz, Darrel Holnes, Julia Griffin, Steve Weiskopf, and all the rest! I'm so lucky to have been your student. Thank you for teaching me how to think.

To all my friends (in no particular order): Ally, Luke, V, Rach, Matt, Dan, Michelle, Sam, Lucy, Keyara, Mere, Katie, Aubrey, Erin, Ariadne, Summer, Emma, Grace, Laura R and H, Emily, Julia, the Bee Hive folks. To everyone who said "Hell yes!" when I told them about this crazy book deal. It all meant more than you know.

To the artists, storytellers, and renegades. Special shout out to Deborah Harkness (who set me on this alchemical adventure), Sarah J. Maas, Dolly Alderton, Elizabeth Gilbert, Samuel D. Hunter, the folks at Dobama/ Southern Rep/New York Theatre Workshop/Playwrights Horizons/ The Public, Richard Linklater, Cate Blanchett, and Krista Tippett.

To Charters, who is currently passed out on my bed and all like, "Why aren't you sleeping yet, human?" and the rest of my furry friends.

And, most of all, to you, dear reader. This book wouldn't exist without you. Thank you for your curiosity and wonder! Kick butt out there!

ABOUT THE AUTHOR

SARAH DURN is a writer, medievalist, actor, and maker currently based in New Orleans. She's written for BUST, Gizmodo, io9, the AV Club, the MarySue, Stage & Candor, and Film Daily, among others, on topics ranging from *Godzilla* to feminism to all things medieval and alchemical. She has acted in regional theaters across the United States, including New York. She holds a BA in collaborative storytelling with a minor in medieval and Renaissance studies from the Gallatin School of Individualized Study at New York University. Now go forth, and kick butt! You got this.